WORLD'S FAIRS

Yesterday, Today, Tomorrow

Roberta Fleming Roesch

Illustrated

The John Day Company
New York

J
606.4
R

Library of Congress Catalogue Card Number: 64-14748

MANUFACTURED IN THE UNITED STATES OF AMERICA

AUTHOR'S NOTE

World's fairs are the stories of the activities of man. They are important events to all boys and girls because, as Henry Ford once said, a world's fair is a place where young people can see how rich the world is in ideas, how much there is yet to do, and the point at which we need to begin.

In addition to the long look at the future and the view of everything new that you get at a world's fair, you see the things that people have known and loved over the years. The oldest of each one of these things is new to each generation.

At almost every fair you can visit there will be great exhibits in mining, farming, machinery, and transportation. There will be children's worlds, foreign exhibits, state exhibits, United States Government exhibits, statues, gardens, midways or entertainment areas, and buildings so new in design they may change future building for many years to come, as designs shown in past fairs have often done.

Not everything about every fair (nor even about every exhibit mentioned) will be told as we visit the fairs in this book. To do this would take many, many books. But, as you read what we have chosen to present about each fair in this book, remember that all these things were probably at all the other fairs, too.

World's fairs have been held in large cities in many countries, but most of the fairs we'll visit in this book will be the fairs that were held in the United States.

A world's fair is never a world's conference table at which countries try to settle their problems. But in its own way a fair brings the people of the world together.

This is important to all of us, too, because the more we know about other countries, the more we understand our world neighbors and why they think and act as they do.

Just as many people have had a part in the making of every world's fair, many people have had a part in making the writing of this book an easier task. It would be impossible to mention here the names of all the people who have helped. I am grateful to each one. But special thanks for special lifts along the way belong to: Miss Ernestine R. Haig, Mr. Guy Tozzoli, Mr. Francis Miller, Marblehead (Mass.) Chamber of Commerce, Edison Laboratory National Monument, Ford Motor Company, Mr. B. J. McFarland, Mr. Harry Collins, Museum of Science and Industry of Chicago, Westinghouse Corporation, General Motors Corporation, Century 21 Exposition, 1964–65 World's Fair Corporation, Belgium Government Information Center, Lincoln Center for the Performing Arts, Mr. John F. Hossenlopp, Mr. W. A. Horton, San Diego Historical Society, Eastman Kodak Company, San Francisco Chamber of Commerce, San Francisco Public Library, American Telephone and Telegraph Company, Illinois State Historical Library, Chicago Historical Society, and, most of all, my husband and children who helped in innumerable ways.

CONTENTS

CHAPTER 1

WHAT IS A WORLD'S FAIR?

A WORLD'S FAIR is a show of shows, visited by millions of people from every land. At night the skies above a fair are painted with rainbow colors. A fairyland of gaiety sparkles with thousands of lights.

Sometimes a fair is called an *exhibition* or an *exposition*. And when you go to visit one you see huge world displays, as many, many countries show the things they're proud of in arts and crafts, science and education, invention and industry, and fun and entertainment.

As soon as you go through a world's fair gate, you feel like Alice entering Wonderland or Aladdin rubbing his lamp. For everywhere you turn your head there are things for you to look at that are never found all in one place except at a world's fair.

You see colorful sights of the olden days, all the best views of the present, and glances into the future that make you stay to look twice.

7

At night skies are bright over fairs.

At the start of a fair, parades march. Flags wave from shining fair palaces. Enormous fountains leap skyward. Bands play. And cannons boom.

Many of the things that are part of our civilization today were first shown at world's fairs. At a fair in Philadelphia, Alexander Graham Bell displayed his telephone. The first escalator people ever rode was shown at a Paris exhibition.

Telegraphs, typewriters, and television were exhibited first at fairs. So were cars, electric lights, ferris wheels, saxophones, home air conditioning, and nylon.

Most exhibitions have a theme — or a special reason or purpose. "Building the World of Tomorrow" was the theme and slogan of a New York world's fair. Usually a symbol is

8

Postage stamps are often put out by countries everywhere to honor the great world's fairs.

built to go with the theme. A pillar and a globe, called the Trylon and Perisphere, formed the symbol for "Building the World of Tomorrow."

All world's fairs take many years to get ready, and sometimes world's fairs open while an important anniversary is being celebrated. A Chicago fair, for instance, celebrated the four hundredth anniversary of Columbus's discovery of America.

Very often great world's fairs are made from swamps or wastelands. Millions of dollars and the work of many hands

Trylon and Perisphere, theme-symbol, New York's fair, 1939–1940

Visitors to the New York world's fair of 1939–1940 were given a glimpse of the future's highway system with this miniature-scale layout. Many of today's superhighways with their complex cloverleaf patterns are now like this.

Courtesy of General Motors Corporation

and minds go into the planning and building of all of them. Often problems, struggles, and dangerous times in history hang like shadows while fairs are being planned and built.

But just as people — in spite of problems, struggles, and dangerous times in history — have always gone on using their hands and minds to make everyday living a little better and to show other people their progress, world's fairs have also gone on to give countries a chance to do the same thing.

Each fair tries to be more wonderful than the last one, too. Many times the world's industry uses ideas from fairs for years after fairs are over. Today's superhighways, with their cloverleaf patterns, were first shown in a model at a New York world's fair.

Often fairs leave a park, building, statue, or theme-symbol behind. The Eiffel Tower, which you can climb in Paris today, was built as the symbol of the 1889 exhibition. And the Museum of Science and Industry in Chicago was once a huge fair palace.

Most fairs don't make money. But trade within countries and with other countries grows because people see new things they want while visiting the fair. Travel throughout the world increases as exhibits and visitors come from all parts of the globe. And, most important of all, while fairs are open, people from many lands are gay and friendly with each other, regardless of where they come from and how they think and live.

For world's fairs take people to paradise. Let's travel to some of them.

CHAPTER 2

EARLY FAIRS

THE first fairs we know about were the fairs in Asia and Africa mentioned in the Bible before the birth of Christ. Many of those fairs were held along with religious celebrations.

In those early days, however, it was hard for people to travel very far, so visitors to those fairs came from one small area. As a result, these early fairs weren't really world's fairs at all. But, as you will soon discover, they played a very important part in the story of world's fairs.

Even though visitors to these exhibitions came from only one small area, the large crowds that attended attracted the traders of the day. And when the traders began coming to the fairs, all the people at the fairs began trading such things as grains, carpets, linens, and furniture.

Little by little, trade grew to be more and more important at fairs until, from those early fairs right up to the

Ancient trading fair

present, trade and industry have been important reasons for any fair or exhibition.

At the same time these first fairs were being held in cities and towns, other early fairs were held along the shores.

In those fairs, called ancient trading fairs, the merchants of Asia, Africa, and Europe sailed from shore to shore, unpacked their goods, and placed the best things they had on the shore. Then, people who lived near the shore came to look at the merchants' goods and showed their own best goods in return.

Sometimes — if you can imagine such a thing — these fairs were silent trading fairs! When this was the case, the sailing merchants went back to their ships after they put

14

their goods on the shore. Then, while these merchants waited in the ships, people living near the shore crept out of the forests, took what they wanted, and left their own goods in return.

After the birth of Christ, fairs began to spring up in many countries under charters granted by kings, and by the time of the Middle Ages (the years between ancient and modern times from 500 A.D. to about 1500 A.D.) people began to travel as much as one hundred miles to attend fairs.

When long trade routes were established in the last part of the Middle Ages, transportation began to progress, too. Because of this more and more merchants, farmers, knights,

Trade routes of the later Middle Ages

from *Your World and Mine* by Dawson, Tiegs, and Adams

lords, ladies, and other people were able to travel farther to go to a fair.

The farmers brought their cattle and grain. The town merchants showed, among other things, their best hardware and cloth. Traveling merchants brought the latest silks, laces, furs, and spices from distant countries. And more people than ever before began to trade with each other.

The week of these fairs usually began with bells ringing and banners waving. People sang and danced, and jugglers and tumblers performed. Everyone was happy, for, in the Middle Ages, many people lived on farms and estates, far away from other people. Their lives were much more lonely than our lives today, and the week of a fair was an exciting time when they could meet and be merry and gay with many other people.

Then, after the holiday week was over, traveling merchants moved on. Townspeople returned to their shops. Peasants trudged to their farms, and knights and lords and ladies rode home to their beautiful castles.

But it was because of the way people liked these early fairs — and because of the way these fairs helped trade — that Prince Albert of England and some of his countrymen got the idea, about three hundred years later, to build the first world's fair.

CHAPTER 3

LONDON 1851
NEW YORK 1853

A GIANT water lily, with a leaf so strong it could hold a little girl, played an important part in building the first world's fair!

When Prince Albert, husband of Queen Victoria, and some other men in England decided to build a world's fair in London to give people from every land a chance to show their best and latest goods, he and the other fair planners ran a contest, similar to some of the contests you may enter at times.

The contest that the Prince sponsored was for a building design for a beautiful fair palace in which to hold the fair. One person who entered this contest was a man named Joseph Paxton who had been a gardener before he became an engineer.

A few years before the contest, a traveler from South America had brought Paxton a huge water lily with leaves that grew five feet wide, a size that's probably wider than

The Crystal Palace, London, 1851

you are tall! Because the leaves looked almost like rafts, Paxton stood his little girl on a leaf one day, just for the fun of it. When he saw that the leaf could hold her, he studied it carefully.

As Paxton studied the leaf, he saw that it had strong stiff ribs, which spread out like ribs on an umbrella. Small, but very strong, cross ribs held the long ribs together and made the leaf unusually strong even though it looked very light.

The more Paxton thought about the contest, the more he decided the design of the leaf would be the perfect design for the fair building, so while he was at a meeting one day he drew his idea for a great crystal palace on a piece of blotting paper. He planned to use a glass roof for the building as well as a huge glass dome that would cover the trees in Hyde Park.

When Prince Albert and his helpers saw the design Paxton drew, they all agreed it showed England's best beauty and art. But when other people heard about the design for the building they were afraid of it. Some said the whole building would blow down in the first strong wind. Engineers warned that its galleries might crash and destroy fair visitors.

But fair planners are men of vision instead of forecasters of doom, so Prince Albert and the other men accepted Paxton's design. When the huge Crystal Palace was finished it was 1851 (18 hundred and 51) feet long, and the year of the fair was 1851. The building itself looked like a magnificent sparkling greenhouse because it was made entirely of glass over a light metal framework.

The date for opening this fair, which was called the Great Exhibition of the Works of Industry of All Nations, was set for May 1, and when the Crystal Palace opened its doors it marked the first time in history that countries had ever come together for peaceful purposes in one building under one roof.

If you had been at the Crystal Palace on opening day you would have seen more palms, flowers, trees, statues, and fountains than you'd ever seen before. And you would have heard young Queen Victoria open the first world's fair.

After the opening ceremony, you and your family would have stopped at booths, such as you see next, and viewed the arts, industries, and inventions that forty countries exhibited.

Of all the countries at the fair, England was able to show the most progress in producing machinery and manufac-

19

tured goods. And, as a result of what England was able to show, some people have gone so far as to say the start of the Machine Age became a part of the world's civilization at the Crystal Palace.

New inventions have always been a big thing at every large world exhibition. And the London fair had its share. A man by the name of Antoine Sax, for example, invented a new musical instrument for this fair, and whenever you see a saxophone you see what Sax brought to the fair.

The United States, a very young country then, was proud to show Colt's revolver, and McCormick's reaper for harvesting farmers' fields. And we were also proud to show our latest and best in false teeth and chewing tobacco!

The arts, industries, and inventions of forty countries were exhibited at the Crystal Palace.

In October 1851, after five months, eleven days, and six million visitors, the fair closed.

Just before the time set for closing, people grew very quiet. Finally, a clock struck. Then, while the clock was striking, all the organs in the palace began playing. Everyone sang "God Save the Queen," and people clapped, cheered, and stamped their feet, just as we do today when we see something great.

After the fair was over, the Crystal Palace was taken down, piece by piece, and rebuilt in another spot, where it stood till it burned in 1936.

Besides leaving a beautiful building for many years after the fair, this first world's fair reached out and touched the future in other ways. With a fund of money that was left when all the expenses of the fair were paid, the Victoria and Albert Museum and other museums and schools were built. A college scholarship fund for "1851 Scholars," which grew from money left over, was begun. And if you were growing up in England now, one of your ambitions might be to be an "1851 Scholar."

Because the fair in London was such a success, some men from New York who visited it returned to the United States with an idea for a world's fair in New York.

The fair which grew from their idea was named the World's Fair for the Exhibition of the Industry of All Nations. It opened on July 14, 1853, with a band playing "Yankee Doodle," as the President of the United States, Franklin Pierce, arrived.

A Crystal Palace with a glass and iron dome, copied from London's Crystal Palace, was built on a piece of land that you can stand on in New York today, when you take a walk through Bryant Park behind the Public Library on Fifth Avenue.

VISIT OF PUPILS FROM THE PUBLIC SCHOOLS OF NEW YORK, TO THE CRYSTAL PALACE.

LESLIE Sc.

Pupils from the New York public schools visited the world's fair in the Crystal Palace, 1853.

Earlier in history, George Washington had stood in this same spot to watch British soldiers land in a nearby bay, and, inside the Crystal Palace, a great statue of George Washington, created for the fair, was one of the works of art of which our country was proud.

You might have looked at this statue yourself if you'd been a New York school child then, for many schools in the city took class trips to the fair, just as you take class trips to many places today. After you looked at George Washington, there were other statues you'd recognize. One was of Daniel Webster. Another portrayed Christ and His Twelve Disciples.

Exhibits such as china, glass, artificial flowers, hats, and wigs showed some of the arts and crafts of 1853. The forward-march of transportation was shown by the latest and best horse-drawn carriages and fire engines. Farm machinery, Taylor's printing press, House's telegraph for sending messages, and cannons showed the progress of industry and invention.

When the fair closed in October 1854, it had not been so successful as the London world's fair. But we must all remember that our country was still very young. And it's fun for us to know about this fair even though it wasn't too successful because it was the first world's fair in America.

The New York Crystal Palace building itself was meant to last forever. But four years after the fair closed, the Palace burned to the ground in half an hour — even though there was a reservoir with 21 million gallons of water right next door to it!

In 1858 the New York Crystal Palace burned to the ground.

CHAPTER 4

PHILADELPHIA — 1876

Y OU and your country are alike in some ways! Both of you feel proud of yourselves when you know you've done something well.

Because our country was so proud of all she had to show for the first hundred years of her independence from England, a world's fair was held in Philadelphia in 1876 to celebrate the one hundredth anniversary of America's Declaration of Independence. And ever since this Philadelphia fair, most world's fairs have celebrated some special event.

This fair was called the Centennial Exhibition, for, as you know, "centennial" means one hundred years. When it was time for the fair to open, the proud people of Philadelphia were even more excited than you are when your birthday comes.

Banners, flags, wreaths, arches, and emblems were everywhere. Streamers of red, white, and blue flannel waved on

President Grant opening the Centennial Exhibition in Philadelphia, 1876

people's clotheslines. Lampposts were painted silver. Some families even painted their homes to look like American flags.

On May 10, when the work of the many hands and minds that had built the fair was finished, a huge parade of soldiers from every country marched from Independence Hall to the exhibition grounds at Fairmount Park.

The giant Corliss Engine, an outstanding exhibit of America's progress in industry and invention, helped open the fair. This machine was a huge steam engine that provided power for all the fair machinery. When Ulysses S. Grant, President of the United States, and the Emperor of

25

Brazil, together, started the engine, the fair officially opened.

People who came to the fair — and many people came by horse and wagon — were wide-eyed at what they saw. Most of them had traveled to Philadelphia expecting to see the Liberty Bell and Revolutionary War exhibits. But, as they walked through the 167 buildings of this fair, they saw that their country, new only a hundred years ago, had grown up and was ready to take its place in the Machine Age of civilization.

When visitors looked at the inventions they saw a refrig-

"The Spirit of '76"

erator car for use with trains, the latest printing press, Thomas Edison's automatic telegraph, and something very new that people called a typewriter.

The exhibit that made fair visitors think they were dreaming, though, was a "talking instrument" brought by Alexander Graham Bell. Visitors buzzed around it like swarms of bees. Some were so thrilled by this telephone they couldn't say a word. Others just looked at each other and said, "It talks. It really talks!"

During the months the fair was held, visitors walked through building after building looking at exhibits. One exhibit that made all Americans proud was a painting called "The Spirit of '76."

A ride in the elevator on Belmont Hill, Fairmount Park; taking a bird's-eye view of the exposition buildings

Brown Brothers

This painting represented America's pride in her land of freedom and liberty. Its life-size figures were three generations of Americans — a grandfather, a father, and a grandson, looking up, with confidence in the future, to the older Americans. You've seen copies of this painting many times yourself, and when you're in Marblehead, Massachusetts, you can see the painting that was shown at the fair hanging in the town hall.

The United States Government exhibit was a place that children liked. Here you could see guns, ammunition, torpedoes, and army wagons. You could also watch rifles and cartridges being made, and you could stand beside life-size models of soldiers wearing every kind of American uniform from the time of the Revolutionary War until 1876.

When your feet got tired from walking, a good way to see the whole fair at once was to take a ride in a special elevator. Elevators were still very new in 1876, but this special elevator, with its large cage and great heavy rope, carried forty people 185 feet up to the top of an observation building. Since the observation building stood on a hill, you could look out of a window and see the whole fair as these fair visitors are doing.

At the end of 159 days the Centennial Exhibition closed. But when everything was taken down, one fair building, which later became the Pennsylvania Museum of Art, was left where the fair once stood.

CHAPTER 5

CHICAGO — 1893

HOW would you like to view a world's fair from the world's first Ferris wheel, in a car as large as a school bus, with bright carpet and soft, plush seats?

You could have done this for fifty cents in 1893, if you'd visited Chicago to attend a wonderful fair.

The fair was the World's Columbian Exposition, held in honor of the four hundredth anniversary of Columbus's discovery of America. And though 1892 was the exact year of the anniversary, the fair was held in 1893 because of the huge job of building it where Jackson Park is now.

One of the tasks in building this fair was finding some exciting new feature that would be completely different from anything the world had ever seen before.

The minds of many men went to work on this. But, in the end, the Chicago planners sent for a brilliant young engineer named George Washington Gale Ferris. When Ferris

The Ferris Wheel, Chicago, 1893

learned that the planners wanted to top even the Eiffel Tower he lost no time in suggesting that he build "The Great Wheel" for the fair.

As people listened to Ferris's plans for a wheel 250 feet high, seven times bigger than any wheel ever known, and taller than any building in Chicago, they couldn't believe their ears. When he said that 36 cars, large enough to hold 36 people in one car, would hang around the rim, everybody warned that no one would risk a ride on such a wheel. The biggest engineers in the country said it wouldn't work.

But Ferris and the few men who believed in him knew that there are always people to tell you something's impossible. So he set out to show the world that the wheel *was* possible.

The world came to look when he finished, too. And so many people took a ride that over a thousand men, women, and children revolved every time the wheel went around.

During the freezing Chicago winter before the fair, many men put their hands to work building the exhibition. When everything was finished the fair was called "The White City" because all of its buildings were made of a gleaming material that shone like marble.

Except for "The Spirit of '76" at the Philadelphia fair, America had not had nearly so much art and beauty to exhibit as the other countries. But, because of the all-white buildings, the great Columbian Fountain theme-symbol,

The great Columbian Fountain in the Court of Honor

Courtesy of Westinghouse

In the Palace of Electricity there were pillars of light, studded with colored globes that flashed out changing patterns.

and the Court of Honor, a whole beautiful story of our artistic progress was shown at the Chicago fair.

The big story told at this fair, though, was in industry and invention because, when President Grover Cleveland, on May 1, 1893, touched the electric button that started the fair machinery, both the fair and the Age of Electricity began.

Many people who visited the fair on the days that followed saw the first electric light they'd ever seen. Children who lived before this time could not turn a switch or press a button, as you do, and have a room light up at once. So, when the children of 1893 walked through the Palace of

Electricity and saw pillars of light flashing out changing patterns, they thought they were seeing a miracle.

In fact, most of the people who saw the Age of Electricity begin at the fair were just as curious about the wonders of electric power as we, today, are curious about the wonders of atomic power. Some people were afraid of it. They asked themselves whether it would be a dangerous toy or a new power to serve man.

In the history of civilization inventions have always come from human needs. The Age of Electricity produced new needs. In order to light the fair George Westinghouse invented a new electric light bulb and developed the elec-

The present-day Museum of Science and Industry that was once the Palace of Fine Arts in the Chicago 1893 fair

trical system most of us have in our homes today. The first electric railway in the world pointed out the progress in transportation.

At this fair you could arrive right at the grounds by trains or steamboats. After you arrived there were many things to see in the state and foreign exhibits. Montana showed a woman made of pure silver. California sent a knight in a suit of armor made entirely of prunes. The new Territory of Oklahoma displayed grasses and corn to show the best and latest progress in farming across southwest America's strip of desert land.

Spain sent a copy of Columbus's flagship, the *Santa María*. Germany exhibited cannons. Brazil showed her coffee industry and served free coffee daily. France built a handsome likeness of the Great Hall of Versailles.

In China's exhibit sat a very wise Chinese, with huge glasses that made children laugh. When you stopped to talk to him he told your fortune for you and forecast your future.

But even more farseeing than the fun fortunes the Chinaman told were some of the serious forecasts of the future that resulted from World Congresses held at this fair. People were looking ahead in those days, just as we are now. And one person at those congresses in 1893 had vision enough to predict that someday there would be aircraft that would speed through the sky at 60 to 80 miles an hour!

Six months after it opened, this shining white fair, which showed the whole world how Columbus's hopes had come true in America, closed. Only Chicago's present Museum of Science and Industry remained.

CHAPTER 6

ST. LOUIS — 1904

IF you've ever sung the song "Meet Me in St. Louis," you've sung a famous song from a famous fair.

This fair, the Universal Exposition of 1904, opened in St. Louis on April 30 to celebrate the one hundredth anniversary of America's purchase of the Louisiana Territory from France.

Although Thomas Jefferson, who was President of the United States at the time of the purchase, bought the land in 1803, the fair honoring this event was held in 1904. Like the Chicago fair before it, it needed more time to get ready.

After six years of work, however, the huge exhibition came alive on the banks of the Mississippi River, on land that was a wilderness only a hundred years before. And for the seven months the fair ran, it gave a dazzling picture of the progress of civilization by the beginning of the twentieth century.

The Louisiana Purchase Monument was both a work of art and the theme-symbol of the fair. Statues of many men you would recognize — Thomas Jefferson, Daniel Boone, Lewis and Clark, Joliet, De Soto, and Sioux and Cherokee Indian chiefs — were everywhere.

The day the St. Louis fair began you would have seen the president of the fair, surrounded by thousands of people, stand beneath the Louisiana Purchase Monument and signal a telegraph operator to inform President Theodore Roosevelt, in the White House in Washington, that the fair was ready to open.

When President Roosevelt got the message he, in turn,

The Louisiana Purchase Monument was both a work of art and the theme-symbol of the fair.

Water cascaded down slopes into pools.

touched the special switch that telegraphed the order to open the fair. As his order arrived in St. Louis, ten thousand flags fluttered from their masts. Water roared down many waterfalls. Fair machinery began to move. Bands played. And two hundred thousand people sang.

Later, as you explored the fair, you saw 1500 buildings, one of which was so large you had to walk nine miles to see everything in the building. This fair, like Chicago's fair, was an all-white paradise, and small waterfalls (called cascades) pouring down slopes into pools, as you see them doing here, made the fair an artistic wonder. At night hidden lights lighted all the cascades and made them moving rainbows.

Two of the greatest wonders which the hands and minds of men had produced by 1904 were cars and airplanes. One of the hundred or more cars exhibited had come all the way from New York under its own power, and people thought that was fantastic.

The "flying machines" that appeared at the fair were considered even more fantastic, however. But air shows and contests were tried out at this exhibition. Often the sky at St. Louis was full of all kinds of these "flying machines" which people called aeroplanes, airships, balloons, kites, and gliding machines.

If you were thirsty, after you looked at cars and airplanes, you could rest and have some iced tea, a brand-new drink discovered by accident at this fair.

While the fair was running, a young Englishman from India ran a Far East Tea House and served hot tea. But the Missouri summer was so hot everyone hurried past the Tea House to buy cold drinks somewhere else.

Finally, the young Englishman knew he had to do something. So, one day, as he watched the crowds go by, he began to experiment with tea by filling tall glasses with pieces of ice and pouring hot tea into the glasses.

He was proud of what he'd made when he finished, and the passing crowds liked the drink's look and its taste. By the time the exhibition closed, iced tea was a popular drink.

After you rested and had something to drink, there were more things for you to see. The wireless telegraph — a newer form of the telegraph than the one President Roosevelt used to open the fair — made a lot of progress during the seven months of the fair. At the beginning of the fair, the crowds thought it was wonderful when the wireless telegraph could send messages between two towers on the fairgrounds. Before the fair closed, though, the wireless telegraph could send messages between St. Louis and Chicago.

Progress in another invention that you use a great deal yourself today was demonstrated at this fair when Lee DeForest showed a radio tube. Later, radios were developed from the tube DeForest showed.

Visiting the exhibits of the latest and best arts and crafts from other countries was like looking at page after page of beautiful colored pictures.

China showed silks, furniture, and a collection of four thousand fans. Brazil showed flowers made from bird feathers, and one flower was a pansy composed of two thousand feathers.

A trip to Germany's Tyrolean Village in the Alps was a journey to an enchanted land. A great castle with towers was surrounded by snow-capped mountains. Another part of the village had tiny houses and a town hall. German bands played, and groups of peasants sang.

Nearly every state in the United States had a building. New Hampshire copied the birthplace of Daniel Webster. Maine had a log hunting lodge. Virginia showed Monticello, Thomas Jefferson's home. The Liberty Bell was in Pennsylvania's building. And New Jersey exhibited Washington's Headquarters at Morristown.

Every world's fair is lots of fun, and this one had fun everywhere. Certainly no visit to it was ever complete without a trip through the entertainment area called the Pike. Here, among other things you could ride a roller coaster, take a boat ride, or watch soldiers pretend to fight a battle from the South African Boer War between English and Dutch settlers.

If you were at the fair on Pike Day you saw two thousand animals and five thousand people from every part of the world march in a parade along the exhibition avenues. All the marchers wore native costumes. You saw tea pickers from Ceylon, candymakers from Persia, carvers from Japan, flower girls from Paris, gypsies from Spain, and silk weavers from China.

In addition to everything else at the fair, this exhibition provided the setting for the world's latest and best sports. As you know, the Olympic Games are great athletic contests to which every country sends its best athletes, and the first Olympic Games ever played on American soil were held in the fair's stadium.

A trip to Germany's Tyrolean Village in the Alps was a journey to an enchanted land.

In honor of this, a statue called "The Victorious Athlete" stood on the dome of one of the fair's buildings. Ever since the fair, this statue has been copied and made into gold trophies of all sizes. Probably boys and girls in your school have received some of these trophies as athletic awards.

December 1, the last night of the fair, came all too soon for the people of St. Louis. That night, just before closing time, the president of the fair rode by stagecoach all around the fairgrounds to the Louisiana Purchase Monument.

Then, standing in the same spot where he opened the fair, he pulled a switch. As bands played "Auld Lang Syne," the lights of the fair went out. While it was dark, fireworks, much like those you see on Fourth of July, outlined the fair president's picture, along with the words "Farewell" and "Good night."

Even when the music and fireworks stopped, however, the effects of the fair lived on. The grounds were restored as a park. Ice cream cones, first offered at this fair, became an American favorite. The Palace of Art was made an art museum.

CHAPTER 7

SAN FRANCISCO 1915
SAN DIEGO 1915–1916

EVEN though World War I had already started in Europe by 1915, two California fairs were built to celebrate the progress civilization had made by successfully completing the Panama Canal.

To make this water link between the Atlantic and Pacific oceans men had battled disease, jungles, rivers, and mountains, so both fairs displayed models of the canal to show the world how truly great the waterway was.

The San Francisco fair, called the Panama-Pacific International Exposition, was a carnival of color with palm trees, flowers, pools, fountains, sea-green domes, and red-tiled roofs. At night the lighting effects were so beautiful the fair was called "The Light Fair."

When the fair opened on February 20, one hundred and fifty thousand men, women, and children who wanted to go to the fair marched through the city streets to the fair-

The Tower of Jewels and the Fountain of Energy, San Francisco, 1915

grounds. When they arrived they saw the first world's fair in America purposely designed to highlight art and beauty, even more than invention and industry.

The Tower of Jewels, the fair's theme-symbol, was also one of its most famous works of art. And its Palace of Fine Arts, which remained after the fair, was one of the most beautiful buildings ever put up for a world's fair.

But even though beauty and art at this fair took your breath away, invention and industry were not neglected. One of the outstanding inventions was the Edison storage battery which could furnish electricity to farms and provide power for farm machinery and other transportation.

Thomas Edison came to the fair himself to celebrate

43

Edison Day. And for this very special day one of the first transcontinental telephone lines was put up between California and New Jersey. This was an exciting event at the fair because in 1915 people could not make long-distance telephone calls all over the country, as we can do now.

When it was time for this event to take place, a great crowd of men, women, and children watched in wonder while Mr. and Mrs. Edison sat on a platform in front of them and placed a telephone call to Mr. Edison's home in West Orange, New Jersey.

While Mr. and Mrs. Edison were making the call from San Francisco, more than one hundred of their friends and relatives, all wearing earphones, were waiting in the Edison home to receive the call.

There was much excitement on both ends of the line when the call came through. Then, after Edison finished talking with his friends, one of the people in his home played a record for him on the latest model of his phonograph. And across America at the fair Mr. Edison heard the record.

A ten-cent ride in a bus that we would consider old-fashioned today took you for a trip through the fair. When you rode to the state exhibits you could see a lump of coal that weighed an even ton in Missouri's exhibit. Then while you were in the New York building you could pretend you were walking through a magnificent Fifth Avenue mansion in New York City, since New York had copied one of these mansions for her fair exhibit.

California had a Spanish mission. A temple of soap was inside the mission and, while you stood and watched, an endless stream of bubbles blew out of it, just like the soap bubbles you blow yourself.

In spite of the problems of World War I in Europe, France built a beautiful copy of the Palace of the Legion of Honor. The Netherlands showed a great clock with a 1500-pound bell. New Zealand exhibited a treasured carved house. Japan sent sacred chickens. China showed 100 tons of carved woodwork made by Chinese school children. And Weather Bureau equipment exhibited by the United States pointed out scientific progress.

On December 4, 1915, the curtain went down on this fair. South of San Francisco in Balboa Park, San Diego, however, the Panama-California Exposition was getting ready to run another year.

A ten-cent bus ride took you for a trip through the fairgrounds.

Some of the foreign exhibits that had been at San Francisco moved to San Diego since that fair was continuing. Because of this, there were many more foreign exhibits for 1916 than there had been in 1915, so the fair's name was changed to the Panama-California International Exposition for 1916.

The whole San Diego exhibition was another showplace of art and beauty. The fair itself was set upon a hill and looked like a walled town of old Spain. Many people who saw its great stone gateway, orange and grapefruit orchards, gardens, and large outdoor pipe organ called it the end of the rainbow.

But even though the buildings — many of which are still standing — looked to the past, the fair itself looked to the future.

There was a reason for this, too, for California, in those days, wanted new people to come to the state to farm. This was very important, because the southwest part of our country needed to develop its farming resources before it could start developing industry.

In order to show fair visitors the good life they could have on a California farm, the agriculture exhibitors were especially proud of their small model farm on which families could make a good living with five acres. Visitors spent lots of time on this farm and they especially liked to go in and out of the little farmhouse that had every city convenience.

While the farming exhibits were being held in one section, exciting car exhibits were being held in another. In fact, progress in automobile transportation was moving ahead so fast that some people were even brave enough to drive to the fair in a car!

Typical car exhibited at the fair

For these people, the fair provided a special automobile field where cars could be parked for 24 hours for 25 cents. And every driver who arrived at the fair after a drive of 500 miles (probably much less than you drive on your summer vacation) was considered so outstanding he got a special button.

To help people get every possible view of the progress of the car industry, there were special car days at the fair. There were roadster days, touring car days, and truck days. There were also head-on wrecks, slow races, and tire-changing contests to show all that could be done with a car.

In one transportation exhibit 18 to 25 cars were put together each day, and children watched by the hour as men started with a rear axle and, little by little, added each part until they built a complete car right while you were watching.

The ice cream parlors in the amusement area were a favorite place with children. And so were the Indian exhibits where you could see Indians weave rugs and blankets by hand, shape pottery and build adobe houses.

Scientists who looked into the future had a part in one exhibit. This exhibit was called the War of the Worlds and was one of the most eye-opening displays at the fair. But, as you learned earlier in the book, world's fairs give a glance at the future that makes you stay to look twice.

And this fair in San Diego — in the War of the Worlds display — foretold a future in which there would be communication between planets within the next few decades, or ten-year periods!

CHAPTER 8

CHICAGO — 1933-1934

IN 1933 and 1934 a world's fair in Chicago was a bright spot in a gloomy world.

At that time the whole world was just recovering from a great depression (a time when people have a hard time to live). Many people had lost jobs, money, and homes. But, as we have seen from the past, fairs go on in spite of problems, so many of the people who needed a bright spot after the gloom came to the Chicago fair, built on Lake Michigan's shore.

Those who were there for opening night saw one of the brightest sights they'd ever seen, too. For at this fair — called the Century of Progress — a ray of starlight turned on the lights for the fair.

At that time a star called Arcturus was one of the closest stars to Earth, even though it was still 225 million million miles away from us. But because Arcturus was closer than

Courtesy of Ford Motor Company

This fair was built along the shore, as you can see from this model of the fairgrounds and a building. A new kind of architecture, such as you see here, was popular at the fair.

many other stars, it gave this fair one of the most exciting opening ceremonies any world's fair has ever had.

When night came on May 17, 1933, a great crowd gathered in the courtway of the Hall of Science, the theme-symbol of this fair. In front of the crowd was a huge lighted panel (something you watch in the same way you watch a blackboard or movie screen to see what's going to happen). A large map of the eastern half of the United States was on the panel.

Four Eastern observatories (places from which men study the stars) were pinpointed on the map. At one of these observatories was one of the world's largest telescopes (instruments used to catch beams of light). The men at this observatory were planning to catch a ray of starlight from Arcturus. The other observatories were planning to help.

As soon as the giant telescope caught a beam of starlight from Arcturus everything was ready for the telescope to focus this beam of light on a photoelectric cell which would, in turn, furnish the electric current needed to light up the fair. When all the observatories were ready, the signal "Let's go" was given.

While you watched the lighted panel in front of you, you saw a flaming circle. And then a star flashed out of the circle!

When this star, for which people were waiting, flashed, the switch for lighting the fair was thrown. A searchlight from the top of the Hall of Science shot a great white beam across the sky. And, as this beam began to touch building after building, the Century of Progress came alive.

One purpose of this fair was to honor civilization's progress in science and industry during the past hundred years, and we shall see some of this progress later in this chapter.

Another purpose, though, was a birthday celebration — Chicago's 100th birthday.

In 1833 Chicago had been a swampy outpost called Fort Dearborn. For this birthday celebration, the fort had been completely rebuilt. You could even go inside its barracks and pretend you lived in those days. You could also pretend you lived in the days in which Abraham Lincoln lived, since there was a Lincoln group of buildings at this fair.

One of these buildings was a copy of Lincoln's Kentucky birthplace. His boyhood home was in the group. So was the store in which he worked and the rambling frame convention hall in which he was nominated for the Presidency of the United States.

In the Colonial Village that showed pages from American history to the world, you would have recognized Mount Vernon, Paul Revere's house, Old North Church, and the House of Seven Gables. America was also proud to show a Pilgrim settlement, the birthplace of George Washington, and the house in which Betsy Ross made the first American flag.

But even though parts of the fair looked like a colored picture of the past, other parts looked like a colored picture of the present. Policemen on the fair grounds wore bright red British jackets, black trousers, Sam Brown belts,

Replica of Abraham Lincoln's birthplace in Hodgenville, Kentucky. The logs and timbers in this cabin were more than 100 years old.

Sky Ride car over the entrance to the Hall of Science

and white helmets. And guides in the children's village were dressed as wooden soldiers.

One of the big things children liked was this Sky Ride. After an elevator trip that landed you on a rocket platform you got into a rocket car and sped over the fair from one tall tower to another.

When you came down from your ride there was lots of adventure waiting in the foreign exhibits. Belgium showed you people blowing glass into all kinds of beautiful patterns. In Mexico's village you saw leather being carved. Costa Rica served coffee and cocoa in a coffee garden.

Italy displayed an antique marble column in honor of Balbo, an Italian flier, who flew from Italy to the fair. Egypt showed an ancient palace. Germany exhibited a copy of the original Gutenberg Bible.

China's exhibit was a beautiful temple, and the craftsmen whose hands and minds created this temple joined 28,000 pieces of wood so perfectly that no nails or other fastenings were used.

In the midst of all the arts, crafts, and entertainment, however, the progress of science, industry, and invention topped everything. For, at this point in the world's civilization, people were beginning to explore science more and more.

One exhibit that showed this progress in science was a balloon with a gondola, in which a scientist rose more than 10 miles into the air. Another exhibit was a steel globe in which a man went half a mile below the surface of the sea. In Henry Ford's exhibit of the Drama of Transportation,

The Drama of Transportation, a collection of 67 vehicles from the ancient Egyptian chariot to the modern motorcar, showing the evolution of vehicles. These are taken from Mr. Ford's personal collection.

Courtesy of Ford Motor Company

you could see the ever-forward march of transportation in an unforgettable way. And, somehow, because you were young and at a Chicago fair, you got a special thrill viewing Henry Ford's lifework and knowing that when he was young and at a Chicago fair, he got ideas — in 1893 — that started his mind working on his future work.

Part of the Drama of Transportation that you saw at the 1933 world's fair was from Henry Ford's personal collection, and all the transportation exhibited showed the world's progress from the time of early Egyptian chariots to modern automobiles.

In the Century Room you saw Henry Ford's first workshop in Detroit, the first car he ever tested on the road, and a machine shop of 100 years ago. Inside of the machine shop four of Thomas Edison's early electric generators, restored to their original condition, furnished light for working.

Because of the great success of the Century of Progress, it ran for two years — 170 days in 1933 and 165 days in 1934.

On Halloween night in 1934, all of the people who had come for one last look knew that as soon as morning came crews of workmen had their orders to start tearing down the fair.

Suddenly, while they were thinking of this in the last moments before the fair closed, the half million visitors began to tear down the fair themselves in order to have something to take home from a fair they'd loved very much.

In the months that followed, crews of workmen finished the job of tearing down the fair. In the end, only two things were left from the fair that began from the light of a star — a sum of money for the study of science in America and the antique marble column that Italy gave to America in honor of Balbo's flight.

CHAPTER 9

SAN FRANCISCO — 1939–1940

Y OU could go to a fair on a ferryboat if you visited San Francisco in 1939 or 1940. Then, at the end of your ferryboat trip, you could visit a beautiful island.

The fair was called the Golden Gate International Exposition, and the island was Treasure Island, a man-made paradise in San Francisco Bay, purposely built for the fair.

The city of San Francisco planned that, after the second year of the fair, the island would become an airport. But, for the two years that the exhibition ran, Treasure Island was to be a holiday land where the world could play together and celebrate the completion of San Francisco's two new bridges — the San Francisco-Oakland Bay Bridge and the Golden Gate Bridge, both outstanding examples of the progress engineering had reached in our civilization.

On February 18, the day the fair began, ferryboat after ferryboat arrived at Treasure Island with people who wanted to help open the fair.

You could ride from San Francisco on a ferryboat and dock at one of these ferry slips at the south end of Treasure Island.

As soon as opening hour came, the Governor of California appeared with a large jeweled key that cost thousands of dollars. With it, he opened a special gate built in the image of the Golden Gate Bridge.

When the fair began, bombs that were like great fireworks started bursting in the air. Bells from the Tower of the Sun began to peal. And, as the flag was raised, five hundred voices proudly sang "The Star-Spangled Banner." Then, when the opening speeches were finished, everyone sang "America" and, with happy anticipation, went through the gate to the fair.

Besides celebrating the completion of the two bridges, San Francisco planned this fair in order to show the world the progress of art and beauty that the Western states, Orient, South Seas, and Latin America had made. Because of this, all the latest and best arts, crafts, industry, agriculture, entertainment, and glory of the Pacific nations and Pacific states were gathered on Treasure Island.

Music played from the Tower of the Sun theme-symbol. Lights danced on buildings along the Court of Seven Seas.

Among the many things to see were rodeos, flower festivals, water sports, fishing contests, wonderful foreign exhibits, and vacation and travel shows.

Across America and the Atlantic Ocean, World War II was to be declared in Europe before the fair was over. Before too many years even the beautiful Treasure Island itself was to be used for America's part in that war.

But people didn't know that when the exhibition opened, so for the time of the fair, music played from a 40-bell carillon in the 400-foot Tower of the Sun theme-symbol. Golden sunlight or magic electric lights danced on the murals, palaces, buildings, Elephant Tower, Court of Seven Seas, and many other courts. And people laughed and played together as they traveled through the festival of beauty the Pacific nations and Pacific states provided.

In the Chinatown at the fair, you saw good-humored Chinese craftsmen working on handicrafts on sidewalks in front of their shops. When you went to the Central American buildings you walked beneath banana palms.

Japan had a very old castle, and this castle was such a work of art that it was completely built in Japan before it was sent to America to make sure everything was perfect. After Japan was sure it was perfect, it was taken down for the trip to California.

When it arrived on Treasure Island it was carefully rebuilt by special Japanese carpenters, proud to have a part in showing the world great Japanese art.

A state exhibit you would have liked was the Oregon exhibit. Here you could walk through an outdoor area and view a miniature dam, Indians, beavers, antelope, and other wonders from the Pacific Northwest.

When you arrived at the Hall of Mines you saw a million-dollar Treasure Mountain that gave you a complete picture of the western mining industry.

At that exhibit you could go into a valley between two tall model mountain ranges. From there you moved on into tunnels and shafts where you saw the inside working of a mine with exact copies of mining railroads, elevators, mills, gold dredges, and California mining towns.

In September of 1940 this island of magic, which had showed so beautifully the glory of the Pacific, closed its golden gates. Only two buildings remained. And Treasure Island itself never became an airport as planned. Instead it became an important naval base which the Navy uses today.

CHAPTER 10

NEW YORK — 1939–1940

AT the same time San Francisco was showing the glory of the Pacific, New York City was showing the World of Tomorrow. And, along with the American flags, New York's blue and orange world's fair flags waved a welcome to people from every land in a civilization afraid of war.

The occasion for this bright and shining fair which ran from April through October in 1939 and 1940 was, as usual, a celebration. This time the celebration was the 150th anniversary of the New York City inauguration of George Washington as President of the United States.

But even though this fair took a fleeting look into the past, it took an even longer look into the future. Its theme, as you've already learned, was "Building the World of Tomorrow."

Like the Chicago fair six years earlier, this fair stressed science and industry as tools for building the future world.

This fair was like a large city. A wonderful way to see it all was a trip by bus.

To preview this future world, America's science and industry introduced at this fair three things you now use all the time — nylon, home air conditioning, and television.

All the buildings and exhibits that you see here were designed to show how man's progress up to the present could improve world living conditions and build the future world. The Trylon and Perisphere symbol in the middle of the fair pictured the world's upward reach to better living.

This fair was held at what is now Flushing Meadow Park. And the story of how the fair was built is another story of people using their hands and minds to show other people what they can do.

In the beginning, the site of the World of Tomorrow was a 3½-mile-long swamp. For thirty years ashes and trash had been dumped in the swamp. There were mounds 100 feet high.

Because the job looked as though it would have no end, many crews of workmen labored 24 hours a day, for nine months, cleaning the dump so they could build a fair. At night men worked by searchlight to drain the swamp, level ashes, build a lake, lay roads and walks, and plant grass and trees.

Then, after all the months and years it took to build the fair, a carnival-colored miracle came alive at Flushing Meadow Park. Two thousand tons of paint tinted striking, modern buildings with deepening tones of many colors. Even flowers were chosen to fit the color scheme. A million tulips and hyacinths, 400,000 pansies, half a million hedge plants, and 10,000 trees added to all the color.

If you attended on opening day, April 30, 1939, you saw a living diarama pass before your eyes. After President Franklin D. Roosevelt arrived, the fair burst into bloom.

A gay costumed parade marched in front of you. Bugles sounded. Bands played. Flags waved everywhere. Sitting on a great white horse was the figure of George Washington who, on April 30, 1789, had been in New York, the nation's former capital, to be sworn in as America's first President.

Behind the figure of George Washington came a living, breathing picture of democracy as we know it in America. People of every nation, every state, every business, and every industry marched. So did the Army, Navy, Marines, and National Guard. And behind it all, marching in their work clothes, were many of the proud workmen who had helped to build the fair.

When the parade was over, the 50-foot statue of George Washington, looking down upon the World of Tomorrow, was dedicated to all the things for which America and the fair stood. After that the man who was dressed like George Washington and who looked like George Washington went through the same kind of inauguration George Washington had gone through 150 years before.

Many of the people who visited the fair during the day stayed on at night. And when they stood by the great Lagoon of Nations that looked like a sea of sparkling jewels, they watched ever-shifting lighting effects of splashing colors and sparkling, skybound fountain and fireworks displays.

Because there was so much to see, many people made many visits to this fair. The shortest way to travel to many foreign lands was to spend some time at the foreign pavilions. For, in spite of the thundering war clouds in Europe that crashed into war the first year of the fair, over 60 nations sent their best arts, crafts, industry, and entertainment.

The British pavilion was so large there were times when 13,000 visitors were in it at once. An original copy of the Magna Carta, likenesses of the royal family's jewels, and nine thousand models of ships belonging to the British navy were on exhibit.

Russia exhibited heavy industry. Belgium showed diamonds from the Belgian Congo. Iceland had a bronze statue of Leif Ericson, and Ireland's pavilion was in the shape of a shamrock.

In the Court of States, most of the states in our country had exhibits of the things of which they were proud. One of the buildings you were sure to visit first was Pennsyl-

General Motors Futurama and general view of the fair

vania's building, a full-size copy of the original Independence Hall.

A transportation exhibit called Futurama was a welcome to the future that most people stood in line to see — 28,000 people a day wanted to get in to see it.

When you got to the head of the line and got into the exhibit, you were given a seat in a traveling sound chair. Then, a moving carry-go-round took·you on a winding trip all over the America that the builders of Futurama forecast for 1960.

In a layout beneath you, the roads of the future, which had once been America's wagon trails, were a miracle scene. Expressways, many-lane highways, modern ramps, bridges, and tunnels were everywhere.

While you looked at these roadways, you also saw a million trees and flowers, rivers and lakes, snow-capped mountains and sunlit valleys. Future factories and farms, cities and towns, a college, an amusement park, and half a million more buildings and houses all passed beneath you as you traveled.

After you left Futurama chances were you went to another building which showed the world the progress we were making in industry and science for the present and the future.

This building had a rocketport in which a gun sent a rocket ship across interplanetary space. And though people in 1939 weren't quite so amazed at this idea as people had been when the idea was forecast at a 1915 fair, many people still called the whole thing fantasy!

As you explored the fair, you probably stopped to see the Singing Tower of Light, with its music and fireworks. For, buried underneath this tower in a container called the Time Capsule was placed the story of our civilization in the year 1939.

Because some of the people living in 1939 felt that, in 5000 years, the people living in 6939 would want to know all about our life in this century, just as we want to know about the Egyptians and Babylonians, a 7½-foot-long Time Capsule made of specially prepared, long-lasting metal alloys was placed in the ground.

Inside the capsule were 35 things that gave pictures of our life in 1939. Some of these things were an alarm clock, a can opener, a doll, a woman's hat, a baseball, an electric razor, a tobacco pouch closed with a zipper, and a knife, fork, and spoon.

Books, magazines, and newspapers as well as complete

information in pictures and writing about our arts and crafts, science and education, invention and industry, and fun and entertainment were put on small reels of microfilm. A microscope for reading the microfilm was included, and there was so much information on the film it would take an ordinary person more than a year to read all of it.

In a quiet moment, instead of in front of a crowd, the Time Capsule was placed in the ground. While a Chinese gong tolled solemnly it was lowered 50 feet to the spot where it was to remain for 5000 years.

A monument was put up to mark the spot where the capsule is buried, and a *Book of Record of the Time Capsule*

The Time Capsule is buried here.

was printed on permanent paper with special inks. Over 3000 copies of this record are in libraries, museums, temples and other safe places everywhere in the world. During the time of the fair you could view an exact copy of the capsule and all the things that it contained.

When you finished looking at this exhibit there were still many things to see. Most children wanted to be sure to see the nightly water show in the outdoor theater, the Boy Scout camp, the Tom Thumb restaurant, and the Penguin Island with real penguins.

All too soon, for children as well as adults, it was time to take the last look at the shining wonderful World of Tomorrow. But, after the fair was over, both Flushing Meadow Park and the outdoor theatre were left as memories of this fair.

The New York City building, built to stay on after the fair, later became the first meeting place of the United Nations in New York.

Beyond this, in the twenty years following this fair, the pictures of the World of Tomorrow, as shown in the roads and highways of the future and in the rocket ship into space, were previews that came true.

CHAPTER 11

BRUSSELS — 1958

WHILE the world's first man-made satellites — as forecast at other world's fairs — were beginning their trips into space, a world's fair was held in Brussels. This fair is important for us to visit, too, because this fair marked the start of the Atomic Age.

At the time the Brussels fair was held, the world situation was called a "cold war." But the atomic power shown at the fair stressed its peaceful use.

All the displays of atomic power, space satellites, and automation (work done by machines that used to be done by people) showed civilization's progress in science and industry since the last fair. An atomic machine, used for atomic power plants, and a clock run by atomic power were in the United States exhibit.

By April 17, 1958, more than seven years of work had gone into building this fair in Heysel Park, five miles from

An atomic machine used
for atomic power plants

Brussels. With 160,000 first-day visitors watching, Belgium's young King Baudouin proudly set off a symbolic flame to open the fair.

Fifty Belgian Air Force jets flew over him while he said, first in one language, then in another: "The aim of this world's fair is to create an atmosphere of understanding and peace." Everything at this fair was spoken and written in English, French, and Flemish (the language used in part of Belgium).

The symbol of the fair was the Atomium, and, after the fair was over, the Atomium was left standing in Brussels.

The Atomium looked like a crystal of metal enlarged 150 million times. It had nine huge steel balls, or atoms, each

60 feet wide. At night, electric lights flicked on and off around these balls. This symbol was over 300 feet high and towered above everything.

Inside the Atomium were escalators and high-speed elevators to take you to the atomic displays in each ball. From big portholes in the balls you could view the fair, and, if you were hungry, you could take an elevator to the restaurant in the top ball.

For many Americans, the United States building, next to Russia's, was the first stop, and we shall spend most of this chapter visiting the United States exhibit. The building was about the size of Rome's Colosseum. It had two floors

The United States Pavilion

Courtesy of Mr. Francis Miller

and forty ways to get in and out. Many people from every nation said it was the most beautiful and most artistic building at the fair.

Some people thought the United States building looked like a candy box wrapped in white and gold lace. Other people said it looked like a bicycle wheel because of the large round pool it had as a hub.

Inside the building, ten 50-foot willow trees grew. Outside were gardens, one hundred and thirty apple trees, and a big pool with a fountain. State flags flew at the main entrance.

At the fair, our country was proud to give the world the feel and smell of America. Because we hoped to show the United States as a happy country in which people had real freedom, everything about our exhibit was made to be like life in America.

When Princess Grace of Monaco, who grew up in Philadelphia, visited the fair, children in the United States building gave her a chocolate ice cream cone to remind her of her childhood in America. Voting machines, suggested by President Dwight D. Eisenhower, and campaign buttons, like those you wear when our Presidents are being elected, showed the freedom of choice we have.

Everything else about our exhibit was planned for a purpose, too. Our Children's Center for boys and girls from four to twelve years old was in our building to show the world America's interest in children.

No adults, except three teachers, could go inside the room where children from all nations played and did arts and crafts together. Queen Juliana of the Netherlands left her children to play with all the other children while she was at the fair.

72

A cutaway drawing of the Circarama Theatre

A streetscape gave a picture of the main street of any town in America. It had shop windows, mailboxes, wastebaskets, traffic lights, parking meters, a newsstand, and a drugstore. The drugstore sold American sodas, hot dogs, hamburgers, and milk shakes.

The Circarama, a fifteen-minute movie of a trip across the United States, was a glistening story of all the things that made America great.

If you had seen it, you would have stood in the middle of a round theatre. On a screen nine feet high, with eleven parts, you would have viewed New England towns, Williamsburg, Michigan factories, Midwestern wheat fields, American schools and school children, Texas cattle, the

Grand Canyon, and thousands of cars on the Los Angeles Freeway.

Then, at the end of the movie, while you listened to "America the Beautiful" and saw New York Harbor, the Statue of Liberty, New York City, Governor's Island, the New Jersey shore, and steamships and tugboats, you would have been proud to be an American.

If you wanted to see something else after Circarama, you could visit Ramac. Ramac was an electronic brain. This means that it was a machine run by electricity and trained to answer questions in much the same way your brain gives you answers to your questions.

Ramac could give fair visitors five million facts in ten languages. People viewing it could go up to the typewriter keys, take any year in history since the birth of Christ, and ask what was important that year. When Ramac was asked to tell the most important thing that happened in 1958, it answered, "The Brussels International Exhibition."

The fifty foreign and eight international exhibits were other important sights at the fair. For the first time in history, the Holy See (which is the governing body of the Catholic Church) had an exhibit at a world's fair. Part of that exhibit was a beautiful church.

Russia exhibited industry and power, models of space satellites, a woman training dogs for space travel, and Russian cars. In Belgium's exhibit were an eight-ton stuffed elephant, interplanetary rockets, and an old town. Children liked Holland's exhibit with its large farm, live animals, and water machine that made waves breaking into foam, such as you see when you go to the ocean.

While the fair ran, each country held National Days. America had Fourth of July for its National Day. On that day young Americans from our armed forces in Europe came to square-dance in bright Western costumes. While people from all the world danced with them, a caller from Texas called the dances.

In addition to the dancing and singing that's done "just for fun" at all world's fairs, recent world's fairs have provided, more and more, a place for the countries of the world to exhibit the finest and most artistic dancing, singing, and drama of our civilization. At the Brussels fair a great World Festival, to which every country could send its best, was held in the heart of the city.

On October 19, 1958, the fair closed. By that day, because of world prosperity, a larger world population than ever before, and faster world travel, 40 million people — the largest crowd ever to visit a world's fair — had come to the first world's fair of the Atomic Age.

CHAPTER 12

SEATTLE — 1962

BETWEEN the 1958 Brussels world's fair and the 1962 Seattle world's fair, civilization's progress in science jetted ahead with a twentieth-century Space Age speed.

In fact, it jetted ahead so fast that, when the Century 21 Exposition was opened on April 21, 1962, to run for 184 days, the purpose of the fair was to preview life in our next century, beginning with the year 2000.

"Man in the Space Age" was the theme of this exposition. Much of the science, invention, industry, and education exhibited showed the many things the hands and minds of men must do in the Space Age in which we live if we are to reach the moon and planets and conquer space for peaceful purposes.

The 600-foot Space Needle, which was over 200 feet higher than Seattle's tallest building, was the symbol of the fair. Its carillon played music that you could hear for ten miles.

Space Needle, theme-symbol of Seattle, 1962

Like the Atomium of the 1958 Brussels world's fair, the Space Needle also had a restaurant at the top. Two high-speed elevators, walled in clear plastic, took you to this restaurant and top observation deck, or to other observation decks along the way.

Every hour the top of the Space Needle, the part that you see here, revolved slowly, as a top revolves — if you can imagine a top spinning slowly. While you revolved with the Space Needle's top, you saw the city of Seattle, snow-capped Mount Rainier, Puget Sound, rugged mountain ranges, and water and lakes.

The Space Needle, though, was only one way to look down upon the fair. On another part of the grounds was the famous Century Skyride. On this you could speed high above the fairgrounds and view everything below you.

There were two million dollars' worth of rides on the Gayway of this fair, and children were thrilled by the Space Wheel and the rocket they could guide themselves.

When you viewed the fair from the ground, instead of above the ground, there were five "Worlds" for you to visit — the World of Commerce and Industry, the World of Science, the World of Century 21, the World of Entertainment, and the World of Art. Boulevards of the World — full of restaurants and shops in which craftsmen sold native products — laced the five Worlds together.

In the World of Commerce and Industry, nations from North America, South America, Central America, Europe, Asia, and Africa showed their present progress in industry and invention and their future plans for progress.

Canada, for instance, showed how she is planning to develop her land in the Arctic Circle and make this land a place where people can live.

The United States displayed electronic cars of the future, electronic-controlled highways, wall-sized television sets, family playrooms that could be changed to atomic fallout shelters, and many other things that showed you what your life will be like in the years ahead.

In the building that you see here, the United States Government presented the World of Science, a glittering spectacular of 1962's best and newest progress in science. The soaring, delicate arches on top of the building were meant to show man's endless search for knowledge. And these arches were considered as striking and new in design as the Eiffel Tower had been considered when it was built for a fair seventy years before.

Inside the five halls of the World of Science there were many things for you to see and do. There was even a do-it-yourself laboratory where young people could work on experiments themselves.

The world's first spacearium — a Space Age way to study planets and outer space — kept you busy for hours in the science exhibit. While you were there you could take a trip through the heavens at the speed of light, and you held your breath while you traveled because the trip seemed so real.

As you zoomed through outer space all that we know about Mars, Jupiter, and Venus was depicted in glowing

The United States Science Pavilion

Courtesy of Century 21 Exposition, Seattle

color as space objects. Planets and stars passed by on all sides and overhead. And sometimes you were so close to them you felt you could reach out and touch them.

By the time you got back to earth again, you may have been ready for another kind of entertainment. But Seattle had that, too, for this was a truly great fun fair, along with its serious side.

The World of Entertainment had puppet shows from Poland, the Royal Canadian Mounted Police, and a color-ful, eye-filling circus. Dancing, music, and drama were everywhere, for countries such as France, England, India, Mexico, Japan, Sweden, China, and Thailand all sent their best to the fair.

The World of Art had one of the biggest art exhibits ever shown in the western United States.

As we have seen in every world's fair, transportation almost always has something new. The "something new" at Seattle was a four-car train called Monorail.

This thrilling transportation of the future had two trains running back and forth on two tracks between Seattle's shopping area and the fair grounds. It ran on a mile-long overhead system, twenty-one feet above the street. Ten thousand passengers an hour could ride on Monorail, and it took only 95 seconds to get to the fair.

No visit to the fair was ever finished until you saw the World of Century 21. This World was the beautiful coli-seum that the state of Washington exhibited. Inside the coliseum was a pearly "bubbleator" in which 100 passen-gers at a time could soar to an overhead floating city of tomorrow which showed how man will work, play, and travel in the Space Age.

Elsewhere at the fair you saw the Plaza of States, unusual lighting that made many exhibits appear to be floating in the air at night, 1000 handmade Japanese dolls, a natural gas clock that had flames for hands, and a 4600-gallon pool of perfume.

Other things you undoubtedly viewed were a 25,000-pound cake with 5000 pounds of decorations (the largest cake ever baked) and a million silver dollars, weighing 63,000 pounds, stacked row on row.

King Henry VIII and his six wives were shown as life-size wax figures, richly dressed in the costume of their day. And, if you visited during Mexico week, you saw 23,000 school children dance real Mexican dances as part of a special pageant.

The Firebird III, a completely electronically controlled car for the Space Age

Courtesy of General Motors Corporation

After the fair the coliseum, the Space Needle, the United States Science pavilion, and 90 percent of the other fair buildings remained. This was something new in world exhibitions, too, since, as you remember, most of the fairs we've visited were torn down at the end of the fair.

But just as lasting as the buildings that remained were the memories that remained from this fair. For out of the things you saw can come new ways of thinking and new ways of doing things that can influence the life of every man, woman, and child on this planet in the century ahead.

CHAPTER 13

NEW YORK — 1964–1965

MANY more new wonders of the Space Age are waiting to welcome you from April through October, in 1964 and 1965, when the city of New York will show the world the first billion-dollar world's fair in history.

The showplace for this fair will be Flushing Meadow Park, the same site used for the 1939–1940 fair. Under, on, and above ground all routes will lead to this fair.

But one of the most exciting routes by which to travel will be the helicopter route! For, even though less than a hundred years ago many children and their families traveled to the Philadelphia fair in a horse and wagon, chances are you'll zip through the sky by helicopter at 155 miles an hour from New York and Newark airports.

Then, almost before you can catch your breath, you'll land at the heliport and view the fair from a restaurant or an observation deck far above the ground.

Heliport and arrival by helicopter

When you're ready to go down to the fairgrounds, you'll ride down in an elevator to a fair that will shine brighter than ever with the progress civilization has made.

During the fourteen months this coming wonderland runs, it will celebrate the 300th anniversary of the founding of the city of New York. And, at the same time that it honors the best progress the world has to show in arts and crafts, science and education, invention and industry, and fun and entertainment, it will also honor our latest achievements with satellites and outer space.

In fact, satellite television may play a part in opening

this fair, for when the curtain goes up on the fair on April 22, 1964, the men of vision who are planning it hope that the opening ceremony will go to all the world by a satellite communication system.

"Man's Achievements on a Shrinking Globe in an Expanding Universe" will be its theme, and its symbol will be the Unisphere, a 120-foot-wide giant stainless-steel globe that represents the world. The Unisphere will be tilted as the earth is tilted. It will stand in the same spot where the Trylon and Perisphere symbol stood in 1939 and 1940. You will not be able to go inside.

But, as you look at the Unisphere, towering 135 feet in

The Unisphere towering 135 feet in the air

Presented by the United States Steel Corporation
© 1961 New York World's Fair 1964–1965 Corporation

the air, the steel strips or links which bind it together will show you how all the world is bound together and how the nations of the world need to live together in peace and understanding.

We need each other for trading such things as foods, clothing, ores, and medicines that we don't produce ourselves. And, with today's satellites in orbit tying us so close that Asia is next door to South America, Africa near North America, and Europe a few minutes from Australia, we need, more than ever before, to live together peacefully.

While you view the Unisphere you'll see the continents and main islands of the earth made of stainless-steel mesh. Mountain ranges will be placed on the globe so they'll stand out and look real. Glass lens, cut like diamonds, will sparkle much as diamonds do, and mark the capital cities of the world. At night, lights behind these capital cities will flash at intervals.

Around the globe you'll see three orbits to represent outer space. A light that looks like a satellite will zoom around in each orbit.

After you see the Unisphere, all kinds of adventures will be waiting, as you begin your trip through the fair. In any direction in which you turn you'll see new things to look at and do that you'll probably never see again, all in one spot, for the rest of your life.

One of the first things you'll want to look at will be some of the pools and fountains that sparkle by day and glow by night. Because of our latest scientific progress all of the changing form and color you'll see in the fountains and fireworks will be turned on and off by electronic tapes. At night the Pool of Industry fountains will change from blue to red.

The Astral Fountain will spout a 70-foot column of water inside a revolving star-studded sphere.

As you watch the fountains, the Astral Fountain will spout a 70-foot column of water inside a star-studded sphere that goes round and round. The Lunar Fountain will have a 25-foot bubble of water that will look like the moon. The Solar Fountain, with its golden bubble of sparkling lights, will make you think of the sun.

Old and new countries from Africa, as well as nations from South America, North America, Europe, and Asia, will all have exhibits that will make you feel you're traveling everywhere in the world. For the second time in this century, the Holy See plans to participate in a world's exhibition, just as it did in Brussels.

Many of the smaller new African republics such as Ghana and Mali plan to have an Avenue of African Nations, and each country will show what it's proud of in its civilization. The Arab states will give a picture of their countries close to the African Street, and the Central and South American countries will have an Avenue of the Americas.

The state exhibits will present a picture of the growth of America. New Jersey will celebrate its 300th anniversary. In Florida's exhibit you'll see real orange trees and tropical plants.

By the time you've visited these fountains and exhibits you may be ready for another ride. One will be awaiting you in New York City's exhibit.

When you go to this exhibit you'll see a 160-foot map of the city. All 790,000 buildings in New York's five boroughs, as well as its streets, bridges, piers, parks, and highways, will be shown. One inch will represent 100 feet on this map, which means that the Empire State Building will stand one foot high.

Above this map will be 50 suspended cars that look like helicopters. When you take a ride in one of them you'll start where Coney Island is located and move around the model by helicopter until you get to Idlewild Airport. A tape recorder and loudspeaker will tell you where you are at every point.

At another spot in the fair, you'll see the greatest concentration of light ever generated. This will take place at a tower of light, the crown of the power and light exhibit.

The center of this building will be an open light court from which three 120-foot-high pylons extend to frame a shaft of light beamed skyward. The source of this beam is

12 searchlights, each producing one billion candlepower of light, and the concentration of lighting you'll see will be equal to 50 lighted Yankee Stadiums or 340,000 automobile headlights. The lights will be seen for miles! Inside the building you'll view a show called "The Brightest Show on Earth."

Part of the fun of any world's fair is eating at the fair! And, if you're in the gas industry's building at a time you're hungry, you'll be able to eat in a restaurant that will have curtains of air for all four walls. While you're eating in this restaurant, you'll get the feeling that the restaurant has neither walls nor doors.

In another part of the fair there will be a World of Food Pavilion surrounded by a world food garden with such things as spices, fruit trees, vegetables, berries, herbs, and nuts from every center of the globe. Inside the food pavilion you'll find snack bars from many, many countries.

As you visit these snack bars you'll be able to eat Boston baked beans, Hungarian goulash, German sauerbraten, Virginia ham, British kidney pie, Swedish smörgåsbord, Indian curry, Louisiana shrimp creole, Japanese sukiyaki, and lobster from Maine.

In still other parts of the fair there'll be 36 million hamburgers and 50 million hot dogs. In fact, the people planning the fair have figured that visitors at the fair will eat enough frankfurters to make a bridge of hot dogs from Flushing Meadow Park to Egypt — and still have enough left over to open up an eating place at the base of the Pyramids.

When you want to make telephone calls at the fair, you'll use a touch-tone telephone in which you'll push a button instead of dialing.

In addition to having fun using these phones, you'll have fun with the family telephone conversations you'll be able to hold in the specially designed family telephone booths at the fair. When you and your family enter one of these air-conditioned shells, you'll be able to sit down together and make phone calls everywhere without using individual instruments.

All of you will be able to talk, just as you do in a family conversation at dinner, and, as you talk, your voices will be sent over the telephone wires through a speaker arrangement.

At the same time that this new world's fair opens, the

Lincoln Center for the Performing Arts, scale model
Courtesy of Lincoln Center for the Performing Arts

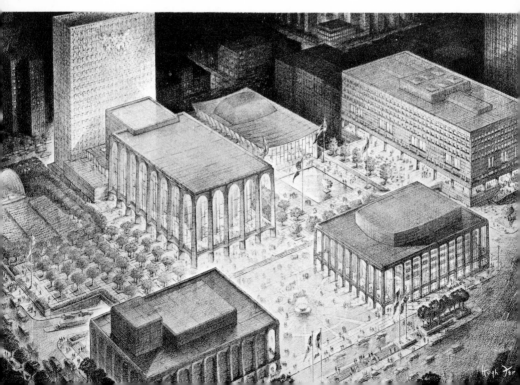

Lincoln Center for the Performing Arts in New York City will also open. While the fair is running, the fair and Lincoln Center will be partners in presenting to all the world people from every land in their best music, dancing, and drama.

People from every land will perform in the outdoor theatre at Flushing Meadows, too, in a giant musical extravaganza that will have the newest sound and listening effects you've ever seen.

A great new stadium will house sports events during the fair, and after the fair is over, the stadium will stay on to be the home of New York's National League baseball team and the American League football team.

One of the most important things you'll visit while you're at the fair will be Futurama II, an even bigger and better exhibit of life in the future than your mother and father may have stood in line to see at the 1939–1940 New York fair.

In another part of the fair you'll see a gay, colorful circus. Old-time circus parades from this show will march through the fairgrounds regularly. In four Du Pont theatres the stories of man's progress will be shown continuously.

Because education means so much to America and our country's children, a Hall of Education will tell the world the story of American education, past, present, and future. Here, among other things, you'll view a School of Tomorrow, an art department of the future, and a Library of Tomorrow. And, because of electronics, the Library of Tomorrow will be an arsenal of information capable of storing and getting information from the world's great libraries and instantly reproducing it, via closed-circuit television, to any school and library in the country.

In New York City outstanding exhibits in museums and libraries will be held as part of the fair.

For example, at the New York Public Library (right next to the site where the first New York world's fair was held) you will see a priceless exhibit called "64 Treasures for the '64 Fair." In this exhibit will be such things as Columbus's letter on discovering the New World, George Washington's Farewell Address, and Thomas Jefferson's draft of the Declaration of Independence.

At the end of the fair, besides Lincoln Center and the stadium, other things will remain. The New York City building, statues, and the outdoor theatre will all stay on in Flushing Meadow Park. The park itself, as well as its neighboring gardens, will be restored more beautifully as a result of this fair. Money left over, after all fair expenses are paid, will be a gift to New York City for an educational fund. And the boat basin, bridges, and new roadways — which were the 1939 fair's Futurama-Come-True — will be more lasting benefits for the progress of the future.

Then, towering above these landmarks, the Unisphere, with all its links of steel, will stay on for all the future to remind us, whenever we see it, that people from all the world have human links between them that can be stronger even than steel.

Men who are building this fair for us have called it, in the words of its head builder, Robert Moses, the "Olympic Games of Progress," to which all the world can send its best and get a chance once again to show how people every-where — in spite of problems, struggles, and dangerous times in history — go on, as they always have, using their minds and hands to make everyday living a little better and to show other people the progress they've made.

The world, far from being finished, is hardly yet begun. And, after all these centuries of progress, there are ways somewhere, somehow, for the lights of our world to stay on.

Maybe a world's fair paradise can be just one of these ways!

The tower of light, crown of the power and light exhibit

APPENDIX
FAMOUS FAIRS AND EXPOSITIONS

1851 — The Great Exhibition of the Works of Industry of All Nations
London, England

1853 — The World's Fair for the Exhibition of the Industry of All Nations
New York, U.S.A.

1873 — International Exposition
Vienna, Austria

1876 — Centennial Exhibition
Philadelphia, U.S.A.

1889 — Universal Exposition
Paris, France

1893 — World's Columbian Exposition
Chicago, U.S.A.

1900 — International Exhibition
Paris, France

1901 — Pan American Exposition
Buffalo, U.S.A.

1901–02 — South Carolina Interstate and West Indian Exposition
Charleston, U.S.A.

1904 — The Universal Exposition
St. Louis, U.S.A.

1905 — Lewis and Clark Centennial Exposition
Portland (Oregon), U.S.A.

1909 — Alaska-Yukon Pacific Exposition
Seattle, U.S.A.

1910 — International Exhibition
Brussels, Belgium

1915 — Panama-Pacific Exposition
San Francisco, U.S.A.

1915–16 — Panama-California Exposition
San Diego, U.S.A.

APPENDIX
FAMOUS FAIRS AND EXPOSITIONS

1924 — British Empire Exposition
Wembley, England

1926 — Sesqui-Centennial Exposition
Philadelphia, U.S.A.

1933–34 — Century of Progress
Chicago, U.S.A.

1935 — California-Pacific Exposition
San Diego, U.S.A.

1935 — Brussels Exhibition
Brussels, Belgium

1936–37 — Great Lakes Exposition
Cleveland, U.S.A.

1936–37 — Centennial Central Exposition
Dallas, U.S.A.

1939–40 — The World of Tomorrow
New York, U.S.A.

1939–40 — The Golden Gate Exposition
San Francisco, U.S.A.

1951 — Festival of Britain
London, England

1958 — Brussels World's Fair
Brussels, Belgium

1962 — The Century 21 Exposition
Seattle, U.S.A.

1964–65 — New York World's Fair
New York, U.S.A.

NOTE: In addition to the fairs and exhibitions listed above, other outstanding exhibitions have been held in such places as Omaha, Jamestown, Dublin, Edinburgh, Manchester, Glasgow, Rio de Janeiro, Milan, Stockholm, Leipzig, Antwerp, Barcelona, Berlin, Florence, Frankfurt, Rome, and other cities throughout the world.

INDEX

WHAT TO DO AND SEE AT THE FAIR

Section 1

Looking Things Over

AS WE SAID in the beginning, as soon as you go through a world's fair gate you think that you're Alice in Wonderland or Aladdin with his lamp. And this is the way that you'll feel, too, when you go to the New York World's Fair to see the biggest exposition the world has ever known.

Chances are you'll look in awe at this Space Age fair, nine times the size of the Seattle fair held only two years before.

On every side as you stand and gaze at the gleaming Unisphere — the largest image of the world man has yet made — you'll start to feel the greatest thrill you've ever had in your life.

In fact, this fair will be so thrilling that the number of people who will journey to the fair is expected to exceed the combined populations of Chicago, Philadelphia, St. Louis, Cleveland, Dallas, Atlanta, Boston, London, Paris,

The Glide-a-Ride will carry visitors from one spot to another.

Moscow, Hong Kong, Rome, Leopoldville, Brussels, Dublin and Glasgow, with every man, woman and child in Greece, the Netherlands, Norway, Sweden and Denmark thrown in. And some people say that to see it all you'll need twelve eight-hour days walking from exhibit to exhibit at a normal pace.

But you won't always have to walk at this fair if you'd rather have a ride.

Instead you can move from place to place by special buses, a Glide-a-Ride, or personal Escorters with sparkling white and gold seats.

On one of these ground rides through the fair you'll want to look only at buildings.

Some that you see will be temples. Others will be Oriental pagodas. And others will be so new in design they'll look like flying saucers, strange crowns, sombreros, or open umbrellas.

Still others — and there will be many of them — will seem to be floating in air. You'll want to notice this "floating" trend, too, because, as you know from other fairs, many of the buildings first displayed at fairs changed the country's building designs for many years to come.

When you've taken a ground ride through the fair you'll want an aerial ride.

For this you can choose the Jaycopter. This modern form of transportation which carries 16 passengers at a time will swish you through sudden turns and dives and unexpected climbs.

The Monorail, on the other hand, will whisk you around a 4000-foot loop at a height of 40 feet. And when you take the Swiss Sky Ride, four rows of four passenger cable cars — two rows traveling in each direction — will glide you

You can view the fair from the Monorail.

Courtesy of American Machine and Foundry Company

around one part of the fair at a speed of four miles an hour at a height of 112 feet.

Later, when you've had this ride and want to ride on a boat, you can go to the new Marina or set out for Meadow Lake. Here you can gaze at fairyland — a fairyland of boats. And when you're ready for a ride you can climb aboard a fancy gondola such as you see in Venice, a riverboat that's a copy of the *Robert E. Lee*, or a glass-bottomed boat that's like the boats you'd ride in the Florida Keys.

Besides these boats you'll also find a pontoon, outrigger, or floating fringe-topped surrey. And when you want real adventure you can take a flume ride in the Amusement Area. Here you'll think you're in the Pacific Northwest as you ride in a floating hollow log that rushes you down a stream through river currents and bends.

When your heart stops beating in double time from this exciting ride you'll find you're anxious to look around for other things to do. But you're bound to notice so many things you won't know what to do first.

All over you'll glimpse man's achievements and see the world's progress again as people from many countries show their arts and crafts, science and education, invention and industry and fun and entertainment.

And the fun and entertainment will take your breath away.

If dancing is your first choice for what you want to do next, you'll see many dancers — including limbo dancers, dancing Indians, and hula and native drum dancers.

Even the water will dance at this fair because, in addition to the fair's glistening outdoor water displays, combining lights, water, music, color, air, and smoke, you'll also be able to witness unusual water formations in a rainbow-

Even the waters will dance at the fair!

colored "Dancing Waters" show. These waters will dance in a building that looks like a quonset hut.

To make these waters waltz for you someone especially trained for the work will push buttons and throw switches on a console that looks like an organ. Then, when this is done, 19 motors will force thousands of gallons of brilliant water through more than 4000 jets to a height of 20 feet. As you watch and hear glorious music you'll hardly be able to believe your eyes as the waters do tangos and ballets.

Besides the dancing at the fair, you'll discover, in other parts, pearl divers, hatchet throwers, log rollers, and glass blowers. You'll also see a hat museum, an ice-cream parlor, an old-fashioned soda fountain, auto thrill shows, and fireworks. Plus this there will be antique car rides, tropical birds, Swiss chocolate making, a working model of America's chocolate center in Hershey, Pennsylvania, and an exciting puppet show where one of the puppets will wear a chinchilla costume worth fifteen thousand dollars!

At other spots you'll stare at the space laboratories and electronic and atomic marvels of "Today" and "Tomorrow" along with all the historical views of "Yesterday."

On State or Special days you'll see all kinds of festivals, concerts, glee clubs, school bands and drill teams. You may even march in a band yourself if your school goes to the fair.

On every day that you're at the fair you'll find ice shows, water shows, stage shows and music-hall spectaculars. And when you go to the Amphitheatre you'll open your eyes to the "Wonderworld" where, on the largest revolving stage in the world, the show will unfold in three parts — the earth, the sea, and the air.

As you make the rounds to these different sights, you'll travel through routes of beauty. And one of the routes you'll travel will lead to the foreign exhibits.

Section 2

Touring the Foreign Exhibits

YOU'LL FIND the foreign exhibits in the International Area. And when you arrive at this holiday land over 50 of your world neighbors will be waiting to show you their progress.

As we learned in another chapter, many of these countries will be the world's newest nations. For them this will be a first time to show their work, their wares, and their culture at a world exhibition. They hope through this to help their trade. And they also hope, as they show their best, that the world will learn to know them and see what they are and can be with world friendship and freedom.

Some of the things these countries will show will be ancient treasures from the Holy Land. When you visit Jordan, for instance, you'll see the Dead Sea Scrolls, as well as the Fourteen Stations of the Cross in stained-glass wall panels.

Later, when you go to the African pavilion, made up of thirteen French-speaking nations, you'll observe a 150-seat tree house restaurant, a theatre, and a live animal exhibit with an elephant ride.

To enter the pavilion of Guinea you'll cross a bridge which will span a moat. Then, in huts that are copies of huts in Guinea, native craftsmen will work on items you'll be able to buy.

The pavilion of the Sudan will be shaped like a mosque or place of worship. And in the exhibit of Sierra Leone you'll learn about that country's romantic customs and see the story of its rise from a slave colony to proud independence.

At the crossroads of the Avenue of Asia and the Avenue of Africa you'll come to the Exodus Pavilion. This building will be covered by rough-cut African mahogany, and the exhibit will show the culture of the Jewish people in relation to the Holy Land. At the entrance you'll view real stones from King Solomon's Mines. A three-dimensional diorama will give you a real-life picture of ancient Biblical days.

Colorful streamers and lanterns will greet you at the entrance to the pavilion of the British Crown Colony of Hong Kong. Later you'll cross a Bridge of the Rainbow over the Lagoon of the Emeralds.

103

While you're inside the building the sounds of Hong Kong will echo through the pagoda or towerlike temple. The pagoda will have a garden, too, and a pool will be stocked with goldfish.

The Republic of China will show its best in a building four stories high, where you can sample Chinese tea and foods after inspecting jade, jewelry, bronze, sculpture, and an art collection dating back to 3000 B.C. India's pavilion will show the country's past and present and have as a special theme "Progress in Democracy."

Pakistan will offer children cart rides and camel rides. Thailand will have a pavilion that's a model of a famous marble temple in Bangkok. And one of Japan's three buildings will be a feudal castle made of beautiful sculptured rock, with a moat surrounding three sides of it.

The Polynesia Village — an exhibit from the islands in the central and southeast Pacific — will quickly catch your eye with its pool stocked daily with pearl-bearing oysters. You'll also gaze at native girls in an exhibit of pearl diving and dancing. At the Indonesian pavilion you'll peek at more tropical wonders, along with native woods and marble flooring.

On another tour of the foreign exhibits you'll want to go to Europe.

Here, to see the world's greatest art, you'll head for the Vatican pavilion which you'll know by its lantern and cross. Inside this building will be Michelangelo's famous statue "Pieta" carved in 1499 when he was in his twenties. This marble statue of Christ, lying in His mother's arms after His death on the cross, will be away from Italy for the first time for this fair.

Other exhibits in the Vatican pavilion will be early sculpture from the Catacombs, a collection of Vatican coins and a copy of the Tomb of Saint Peter.

The largest exhibit in the International Area will be the Belgian Village. Among the more than 100 typical Belgian buildings in the village's 17 colorful blocks will be a Gothic church, town hall, pigeon tower, fish market, and many shops.

At the Spanish building, you'll see a cornerstone brought from Spain from the monument of Queen Isabella. And in the Irish exhibit you'll look at the origins of the Irish language and its development.

Michelangelo's famous "Pieta"

To make everyday living brighter and better, Denmark will display furniture, china, and silver. It will also have a playground especially for children. West Berlin will have as its building a perfect cylinder, topped by an unusual canvas tent roof.

From the land of William Tell and Heidi — Switzerland — there will be a collection of historic clocks. Among them will be ancient sundials, a Roman water clock, early alarm clocks, rare hourglasses — and an atomic clock that's the latest scientific creation. There will also be a watch display and a Swiss Shop with music boxes, cuckoo clocks, and wood carvings.

The Austrian pavilion will be an A-frame building made of wood to show the country of Austria as a land of mountains and timber. The French pavilion will have, among its 200 displays, a million-dollar model of Paris. As you watch it you'll see the model change to show the lights and sounds of the city from dawn till night.

The International Plaza, located near France's exhibit, will be a fair within a fair and a United Nations of people. The sixteen separate buildings will house the exhibits of countries and organizations without pavilions of their own, and as you roam through this area you'll catch sight of many lands.

When you're ready to investigate something else, you can visit the Central America-Panama pavilion, which will look like six native sombreros. At night great shafts of light will shoot skyward through the tops of these sombreros making them look like volcanoes in Central America. While you're going through this pavilion a mural of the Pan American Highway will be an eye-catching scene.

In the Mexican pavilion you'll see Mexican-made crafts

and the country's latest progress in industry, housing, education and culture.

As you say goodbye to Central America you can say hello to South America. Here you'll visit Chile and see nitrate, copper, and fish products. Argentina will roast whole steers on a large wheel rotisserie to show her beef-exporting industry. And Venezuela will have such a rich display of tropical plantings you'll think you're in that land itself.

Section 3
Taking in More Sights

WHEN YOU feel like looking at other things besides the foreign exhibits, Sinclair Oil's Dinoland will be a good place to go. Here prehistoric dinosaurs of 160 million years ago will open your eyes in amazement.

During the age in which dinosaurs lived the crude oil of today (which supplies our petroleum products) was mel-

International Plaza, a fair within a fair

Courtesy of International City, Inc.

lowing in the earth. Because of this, Sinclair Oil created for the fair nine life-size fiberglass models of the dinosaurs living then.

The models were built in Hudson, New York, and when they were ready for the fair they floated down the Hudson River on an enormous barge. When you view them at their exhibit, they'll be in a garden setting that will give you a picture of geology in prehistoric days.

The largest dinosaur you'll see will be the Brontosaurus (Bront-o-SAWR-us) who lived in North America and was known as "Thunder Lizard." This gigantic plant-eating dinosaur weighed about 20 tons and was over 70 feet long. Supposedly the ground shook whenever the dinosaur walked.

After you've seen this world of the past you can leave for the Space Age world in General Motors' welcome to another new future. Here Futurama II will be an even greater show than Futurama I. And when you take the pulse-throbbing ride through life on this planet and in outer space, remember that Futurama I came true in twenty years.

After the Futurama, a different kind of exhibit will be the wax museum where fifty famous figures, outstanding in their lifelike look, will be housed. They are valued at over two million dollars. Among the figures you'll observe will be Jesus and His Disciples at the Last Supper, Joan of Arc, Pope John, Pope Paul, Marie Antoinette, Cleopatra, John F. Kennedy, Dwight D. Eisenhower, and Cardinal Spellman.

Another sight you won't want to miss will be the nation's largest closed-circuit television network.

Here, in the Radio Corporation of America building, you'll be able to see how a color TV show is put together.

One of the nine life-size models of dinosaurs created for the fair

Children viewing the Brontosaurus

You'll also see what you look like when you're on television yourself.

The next thrill for you and your parents will be Ford's Magic Skyway ride, where you'll travel from the Stone Age to the Space Age in Ford-built automobiles. This trip, from the dawn of history to the world of tomorrow, will last for half an hour and while you're a passenger on the ride, you'll travel through the kind of tunnels that will make you feel you're breaking through both time and sound. The building in which you'll take the trip will be seven stories high and three football fields long.

When you visit the Bell System's building you'll see a floating structure that looks like a giant flying saucer.

Once you're inside of this building, armchairs will take you for a ride that will show you the invention and industry behind telephones, telegraphs and other message-sending systems. During the 50 scenes of the ride you'll see how

In Futurama II you'll ride into tomorrow and have a world-wide adventure.

Courtesy of General Motors Corporation

Courtesy of Ford Motor Company

The Ford Pavilion will be the largest aboveground building on the fair-grounds.

In this "floating" building that looks like a giant flying saucer you'll see the growth of man's activities in communicating with others.

Courtesy of American Telephone and Telegraph Company

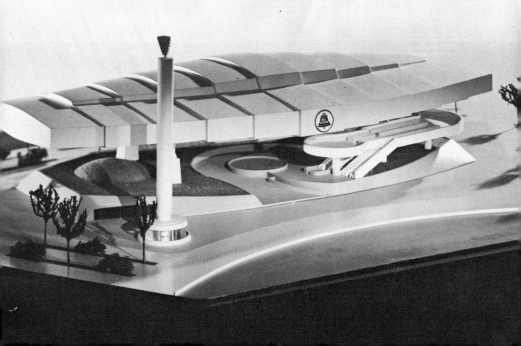

The Revolutionary War will come to life in this shadow
box exhibit.

man's activities in communicating with people have grown
from the past's primitive drum signals to today's global and
space networks.

At another part of this building you'll see the future, too,
in working models of new telephones. You'll even see video
telephones which, like your family's TV set, will provide
both pictures and sound.

When you want to switch from the future back to the
past again, the Continental Insurance Company will bring
the Revolutionary War to life. In this building, that will
look like a shadow box, you'll hear a lot of folk songs, and on
an outdoor screen you'll see a perfect image of the first
double-barreled rifleman in history as well as a picture of
the only woman to enlist as a man in the Continental Army.

Once you're inside of the building you'll be in 1776 as

you watch in-the-round dioramas of the winter encampment at Valley Forge and the battles of Bennington, Saratoga, and Bunker Hill. You'll also see such "living" sights of Paul Revere, John Paul Jones, and George Washington you'll almost think you can talk to them.

Speaking of pictures, however, Kodak's exhibit at the fair will present a world of photography that's the greatest you've ever seen.

To prepare for this world of photography a Kodak Photo Caravan traveled for over a year to take breathtaking pictures of the beauty and drama of life. You'll see these pictures at the fair in a tower of photography. And you'll know this tower of photography by the five giant photos around it. These will be the largest prints the world has ever seen.

From the top of the Kodak building you'll be able to take your own shots of what will look like a trip to the moon. And elsewhere you'll find other views if you want to use your camera.

When you're ready to look at another sight — the magical "Man on the Moon" show — keep your eyes wide open for a building with a moon dome that looks like a part of the satellite's surface. This will be the Pavilion of Travel and Transportation. In addition to the "Man on the Moon" you'll find a Transportation Hall of Fame as well as marvelous displays of man's industry and invention in air, car, marine, and space travel.

Science and education will both be at this fair.

New York City's Hall of Science, for instance, will show man's achievements in this field, while the Hall of Education will show what our schools are doing. Besides the sights we mentioned in an earlier chapter, the glowing Hall

Courtesy of
Continental Insurance
Companies

A craftsman finishing an in-the-round diorama

The tower of photography and the world's largest photo prints

Courtesy of Eastman Kodak Company

A merry-go-round of bright horses will be at the Festival of Gas.

of Education will have a gallery of "moving walls" showing life-size copies of the greatest paintings in the world.

Plus this you'll see a children's world, toy fair, teen-age lounge, human brain, and electronic brain. You'll also see the story of reading and writing, an automatic answering service for questions, an automated school lunchroom, and an exhibition of pilots being trained for outer space.

In New York City's Hall of Science you'll see rocket and space exploration displays, and over your head you'll view a simulated (or "pretend") meeting of two full-sized manned orbital vehicles. As you watch, the vehicles will move down so you can inspect them closely.

During one of your trips to the fair save time for the Festival of Gas.

You'll know this building when you see it by the merry-go-round of bright horses moving around the outside. Later,

A general view of the fair, scale model

when you go inside, you'll move upward on a moving ramp to watch the exhibits below as a slowly revolving ring passes the huge prancing horses. This building will have a Fun House, too. And you'll also want to take a look at its puppet theatre and magic show.

Section 4
Eating and Snacking at the Fair

IT'S EASY to work up an appetite while visiting a fair! But, at this fair, as at all fairs, you'll find lots to eat.

In fact, as you eat your way through the grounds you'll be learning in a wonderful way where the world's food comes from and how world neighbors eat.

There'll be your American favorites, of course, in the miles of hot dogs and hamburgers available at the fair. And there'll also be the sandwiches that you like most for lunch.

But when you want a new treat and a new kind of sandwich to eat, the Seven-Up pavilion will be the kind of adventure you've never had before. You'll find international sandwiches here from spots all over the world, and when you've chosen what you want, you'll eat your meal at a table covered by 20 overhead shells.

At other times you can have meals at some of the foreign pavilions.

France, for instance, will serve French food in a copy of a Paris restaurant. Chile will give you seafoods. And while you're seeing Belgium you can eat waffles and pastries on an outdoor terrace.

At one of Japan's exhibits Japanese dishes will be prepared and served by geisha girls. And at Argentine's exhibit you'll have the Argentine version of our country's barbecues.

Sweden will bring to this world's fair the colorful, exciting smörgåsbord for which it was so famous at the last world's fair in New York. A chalet restaurant will be Switzerland's treat. And in the International Plaza you can sample different foods from 15 to 20 nations.

When you've had your fill of foreign food and want to try something else, the glass-enclosed Top of the Fair restaurant will give you a majestic sight. You'll find this restaurant right below the helicopter landing port where, as you learned in a previous chapter, helicopters from nearby points will bring you to the fair.

For another meal and experience you can eat in beauty in the Restaurant of Tomorrow. Here you'll sit at a table by a lovely cascading fountain. Radiant gold and silver trees will surround you while you eat.

When you want to turn back history and eat in the olden

days, look for Little Old New York. Or, if it's Chinese food you want, set out for the Chun King Inn, where, for less than a dollar, you'll eat a seven-variety Chinese meal in a teahouse in an Oriental garden. Waitresses in Chinese dress will serve your food from rickshaws.

The Greyhound Post House, a forecast of tomorrow's bus terminal restaurant, will give you the kind of down-to-earth meal you'd eat on Main Street, U. S. A. And when you're in the Hawaiian exhibit you'll see an expensive but beautiful spot where a hundred gas-fired luau torches will make you believe you're in Hawaii.

You'll eat an entire luau here, and while you eat this three-hour meal you'll be surrounded by native customs. You'll also see a young pig roasted on hot bricks, exactly as pigs were roasted when the first missionary landed on Oahu.

West Virginia will have a mountain lodge where you'll eat golden trout. And Louisiana will serve the food that you'd eat in the famous French Quarter if you were in New Orleans. These last two are in state pavilions which we'll be touring next.

Section 5
Seeing the Sights in the Government and State Pavilions

WHEN YOU'RE READY to take a look at the sights in the United States Government pavilion you'll see another structure that looks as though it were floating.

This twelve-million-dollar building — larger than a city block and as long as two football fields — will be a striking example of Space Age building trends. When you walk into the building, the largest our country ever built for any world exposition, you'll see a bright and glorious view of all we can accomplish with freedom and democracy.

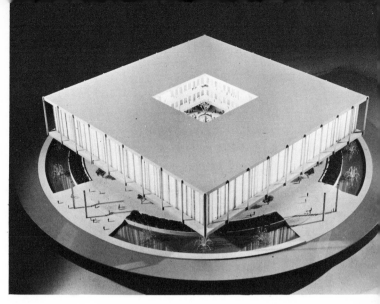

A model of the twelve-million-dollar United States Government pavilion

One of the things that you'll approach, and probably try out, will be another armchair ride in which you'll travel through sights and sounds intended to show to all the world the best of America.

After you've taken this armchair ride and rested in the government's garden court, you may want to leave the building to visit the state exhibits.

Among the many different states bringing their best to the fair will be New Jersey. Here in its 21 plastic tents — one for each of its counties — the garden state will celebrate its 300th anniversary.

New York will also have a tent — a 100-foot-high Tent of Tomorrow — which some people call the descendant of the canvas tent of yesterday.

While you're inside of this new kind of tent you'll notice an elevator that looks much like a copy of a Space Age vehicle. You'll be able to ride this vehicle right to the top of a tower, and when you shoot to the tower's top you'll be at the highest point at the fair.

"Miniature America" will be Missouri's exhibit. Here a main attraction will be the *Spirit of St. Louis*, the airplane made famous by Colonel Charles Lindbergh's transatlantic flight. You'll also see a showing of the latest in space vehicles.

Time will turn back a little in Maryland's exhibit while you watch in a moving film Francis Scott Key write "The Star-Spangled Banner" during the War of 1812 while the bombs burst in the air.

In the West Virginia exhibit you'll take a trip through a coal mine. You'll also stop to have a look at a radio astronomy sky exhibit, since the world's largest radio telescope is located in West Virginia.

Alaska, a newcomer to the states since the last New York world's fair, will show a glittering model of the twinkling northern lights (the famous aurora borealis). This state will also show you its totem poles and polar bears.

In the Illinois pavilion "Great Moments with Mr. Lincoln" will be a sight to inspire you for all the rest of your life. And when you stand by Walt Disney's figure of Abraham Lincoln you'll have a page for your memory book that you may never forget. You will also see the Illinois-owned historic manuscript of Lincoln's Gettysburg Address.

At the Minnesota exhibit a fishing and outdoor living area will be waiting for your visit. Montana will display a centennial train that traveled across the country, and one of the things you'll want to see here will be a million dollars in shimmering gold nuggets.

In the joint exhibit of the six New England states you'll think that you're in New England when you see the enchanting country store and the quiet village green.

120

A copy of a Hollywood landmark — Graumann's Chinese Theatre — will greet you at California's exhibit. This, as you know, is the well-known spot where many of the world's famous actors and actresses leave their famous footprints. Copies of many footprints will catch your eye at this building. Once you're inside of the building you'll have a look at movie sets and see a movie being filmed.

Texas will tell its story through a series of pavilions and a great Music Hall. And the cheesemakers of Wisconsin will exhibit for their state the largest piece of Wisconsin cheese the state has ever produced.

In another part of the exposition — the Lake Amusement Area — Florida and Hawaii will have their state exhibits.

A 100-foot Citrus Tower will be the Florida marvel, and on top will be an orange that's 15 feet in diameter. You'll also see at this exhibit an amusing live porpoise show, the first of its kind ever seen at a world exhibition.

Hawaii, another newcomer since the last fair in New York, will show at this exhibition a copy of the islands in a miniature ocean. Besides this, you'll see an island village, showing Hawaiian thatched huts and picturing life in old Hawaii.

Section 6
Doing and Seeing Still More

NO ONE can take in everything on one trip to this fair! But be sure on one of your trips through the grounds to see the imposing copy of Columbus's flagship, the *Santa María*.

You'll be able to walk through a wharf to this ship and as you go through the walkway you'll almost think you're living in 1492.

Once you set your feet on the ship and see the colorful likenesses of the men who worked as Columbus's crew you'll have a living picture of how the "spacemen" of yesterday lived throughout this voyage.

As you leave the *Santa María* and are ready for something else, head for the General Electric building.

This will lead to Progressland, and as you go through Progressland on another armchair ride 50 scenes of progress will be brought to life for you by many of your favorite Walt Disney characters.

When you want to see the progress we've made in scientific advances, the National Cash Register pavilion will be the spot for you. This will be one more structure that seems to float in the air. And during the time that you're inside you'll see the possibilities of the microworld beneath our view.

Just as one example of the things beneath our everyday view, you'll be able to take an unbelieving look at the entire contents of the King James' Version of the Bible reduced to a size so small that it fits on a small file card. But, viewing it through a microscope, you'll see every word. You can also go to a game room, while at the exhibit, and operate and match your wits with the latest business machines.

While your interest is still with scientific progress go to the IBM building.

Here you'll be seated in a section, somewhat like a theatre, in which you'll be lifted by hydraulic jacks 53 feet up into an "information machine." The "machine," a 90-foot theatre, will show how computer systems solve our everyday problems.

After you've viewed this scientific progress you can go on a cruise.

This will be a special cruise, too, in the Pepsi-Cola-UNICEF pavilion where the story of all the world's children — their songs, their laughter, and their needs — will be the highlights of the cruise.

As you view the building which houses the cruise you'll see a 124-foot Tower of the Four Winds. This will perform like a giant mobile, and more than 100 colorful symbols and copies of birds, fish, and animals will spin and turn in the breeze.

Once you're inside of the building you'll take a trip around the world, as you cruise through Walt Disney's version of the British Isles, Europe, the Mediterranean countries, Africa, the Middle East, the Far East, and South and Central America. As you cruise by the Eiffel Tower, the Taj Mahal, Victoria Falls, and many other places you'll be entertained along the shores by life-size figures of costumed children acting, dancing, laughing, and singing in many different languages.

While you're thinking about the world's children and how we're all bound together you may want to think about pen pals, too. And there'll be a place at the fair for that — the largest pen pal project in history.

To be a part of this project — in the Parker Pen exhibit — you'll have to fill out a card, giving your age, sex, address, and hobbies. Then, when a computor matches it with a name from another country, you can write to your pen pal on a postcard from the fair.

Another special favorite of yours — the Coca-Cola Company — will present as its fair exhibit a 610-bell carillon, the largest carillon in the world. As the musical voice of the exposition, the bells will strike the time of day and play music from 120 countries.

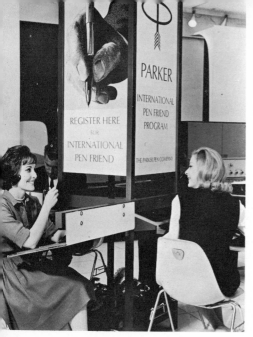

You may pause in your sight-seeing to write a pen pal in some distant country.

Since religion has always had a place in the history of civilization, some of the world's religious faiths built buildings for this fair. This is another world's fair first. As you visit their buildings you can think about God awhile as art, films, gardens, music, pools, and science make Him real to you.

In addition to the Vatican pavilion you'll find a Protestant Center, lighted day and night by a gleaming cross. Billy Graham has a building, too. And when you see a seven-pointed star you'll be at the Christian Science pavilion.

Besides these exhibits of the world's religions, the Mormon Church will have a structure with towers that are perfect copies of the east spires of the famous Salt Lake City Temple. And through sermons and films on the atoms, creation, and space, another exhibit called the "Sermons from Science Pavilion" will attempt to show how science and God are closely tied together.

To turn from the serious part of the fair to one of the biggest fun spots, you'll want to find your way to the United States Rubber Company's 80-foot-high giant tire. People can ride in this tire which looks like a Ferris wheel, and when you take your turn in one of the 24 barrel-shaped gondolas around its circumference you'll have a high, clear view of the fair.

Whether or not you're a Girl or Boy Scout, you'll like the Boy Scout pavilion — "The Wonderful World of Scouting." Boy Scouts from everywhere in the land will visit this building at the fair, and special corps of volunteers will help with fair activities and aid handicapped and aged visitors.

In addition to what we've mentioned here, there'll be many other things.

There'll be many sports, for instance, both in the new Shea Stadium and the World's Fair Arena. And if you're

You can ride on this giant tire which looks like a Ferris wheel.

Courtesy of
United States Rubber Company

Before your fair journey ends visit this Time Capsule pavilion.

visiting the fair during some of the tryouts for the next
Olympic games you can witness the tryouts held at or near
the fair.

The American Indian pavilion will be another world's
fair first, because for the first time in history America's first
settlers will display an organized exhibit at an international
exposition. You'll see the braves practicing archery here at
the same time the squaws prepare smoked salmon.

At another part of the fair, you'll see the Demograph, a
45-foot electronically controlled map of the United States
of America in which every birth, death, immigration, and
emigration will be recorded.

When you want to mail a postcard, you'll go to a special
World's Fair Post Office, built to serve people from many
lands. After you've finished your business you can stay on

126

for a while, in an open spectators' gallery, where you'll watch the handling of mail while the process is explained.

At the only hill site at the fair you'll see the special World's Fair House. And in another part of the fair there'll be the special World's Fair Terminal.

This will be the Eastern Airlines exhibit and also serve as a station for the right-to-the-fairgrounds bus shuttle that the airline will provide from LaGuardia and Idlewild airports for visitors who come to the fair from the cities served by the airline.

Before your fair journey is ended you'll want to make a special trip to the Westinghouse exhibit.

Here you'll see a new Time Capsule, ready to be buried at the end of the fair, right beside the original capsule that told the story of civilization at the time of the last New York world's fair.

This capsule, made of super-stainless steel, will tell the people of 6939 what man has done since 1939. Among the things it will record will be full information on atomic power, wonder drugs, jet aircraft, World War II, the United Nations, the four-minute mile, and the discovery of the Dead Sea Scrolls.

And when it's buried at the end of the fair to tell the story of people in our great universe, so will this brilliant and shining fair have told the story fairs always tell and have shown that, despite world problems, man goes on with his hands and mind showing and sharing his best.

In fact, more than ever, this Space Age fair will have shown what man can do when people, in understanding and peace, share together the progress they've made!

Index

Date Due

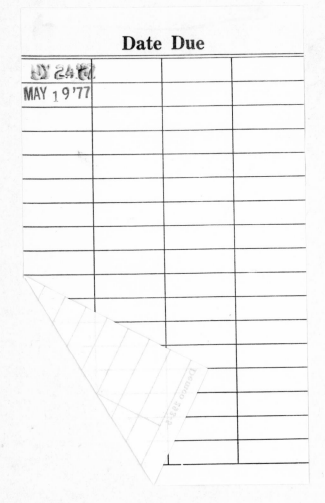